THE PEOPLES TRIBUNAL
of IRELAND

INDEPENDENCE, IMPARTIALITY, INTEGRITY

THE PEOPLES TRIBUNAL OF IRLEAND
– Handbook v 1, 2020 –
ISBN-13: 978-1-906628-91-8
Published by CheckPoint Press, Ireland.

www.checkpointpress.com

CONTENTS

This book is available worldwide as a POD title online – or from your local bookshop by quoting the ISBN on the previous page. It has been priced so as to be affordable for all.

Bulk orders (of 10+ copies) may be sourced at 10% discount directly from 'bookstore@checkpointpress.com'.

INTRODUCTION

This handbook has been produced as a foundation guide to the formation, structure and operations of the Peoples Tribunal of Ireland ('PTI') which came into being on July 1st 2020.

The contents herein are subject to revision and amendment by majority vote of the PTI Council at any time* (*after the 12-month initiating phase which will be directed by the Executive) in line with Tribunal Rules and after putting the issue (if required) to the PTI Panel and/or in consultation with PTI Operations Officers.

Accordingly, this handbook serves only to compliment the authority of the elected PTI Council. In the event of any conflict between the contents of this handbook and any formal decision or declaration of the elected Council, the decision of the elected Council has priority.

Subject to any such authorised revision(s), the terms of this guidebook will in the interim serve as; (i) the rulebook, (ii) the constitution, and (iii) the operations manual of the Peoples Tribunal.

For ease of reference and understanding the relevant Sections are arranged by numbered Articles (i.e. by numbered paragraphs). Any amendments, alterations or additions to this original text will be incorporated into the main text in future printings under sub-paragraphs with the same initiating Article Number (e.g. 1a, 1b, 1c etc) to include a reference to whichever Council altered or amended the original text.

PTI Executive July 2020

THE PEOPLES TRIBUNAL
OF IRELAND

INDEPENDENCE, IMPARTIALITY, INTERITY

*Mission Statement

(i) **The Peoples' Tribunal of Ireland** is an initiative by residents and citizens of the Irish State to lawfully address persistent, widespread, endemic lapses and failures of the Irish State to adhere to the Rule of Law in respect of fundamental human rights, and in particular to provide for the individual's right to access justice.

(ii) **To provide for** the impartial and objective assessment and/or investigation of issues, events, actions, questions, enquiries and/or cases which are pertinent to the constitutional integrity of Irish society and to the lawful status of sovereign Irish people.

(iii) **To provide** some manner of authoritative, documented redress for aggrieved citizens and residents which is; (a) honest, fair, objective and impartial; (b) that is independent of government and vested interests; and (c) which is constructed and composed in express alignment with internationally-recognised human rights law and with EU and domestic law, in strict order of legal precedence according to existing positive law.

(iv) **To aid in the determination of legal certainty** by providing for the production and publication of qualified written mandates in the form of PTI Judicial Orders, Rulings, Findings Directives and/or Decrees to be binding on the parties served, according to the Rule of Law.

(v) **To provide for a People's Prosecution Service** in support of the individual's right to initiate and prosecute criminal proceedings in the Irish Courts under *S.10 of the Petty Sessions (Ireland) Act 1851* and to provide for the active and effective implementation of existing citizens' arrest powers as laid out under *S.4 of the Criminal Law Act 1997*.

(vi) **To provide for independent, qualified arbitration and mediation services.**

(vii) **To provide an open public forum** for residents, citizens and all interested parties to contribute to and learn from the collective experience and expertise of the PTI Membership, in open collaboration with any and all other relevant, pertinent or applicable sources, resources, groups or institutions – whether statutory, private, independent, incorporated or unincorporated – for the purposes outlined herein.

All, as subject to amendment by the elected PTI Council. *

Abbreviations / Short Forms

PTI = Peoples Tribunal of Ireland

Executive = Chairperson, Secretary & Treasurer

PTI Admin = Council + Operations Officers + DCO

DCO = Data Control Officer aka 'Aide to the Executive'

I.D. = Investigations Division

A.D. = Adjudicating Division

P.D. = Prosecutions Division

OO = Operations Officers

PTI Panel = All signed-up PTI Members

GS = General Submission (question, topic, issue etc)

CS = Case Submission

CRF = Case Reference Number

PO = Proposing Officer (any member of PTI Admin)

SC = Sponsoring Councillor

SCF = Submissions Cover Form

QM = Quarterly Meeting

AGM = Annual General Meeting

ECM = Emergency Council Meeting

EGM = Emergency General Meeting

CS website = Case Submissions website

PTI website = www.peoplestribunalireland.com

MCH website = www.mycasehistory.com

OVERVIEW OF PTI OPERATIONS ACCORDING TO THE RULE OF LAW

JURISPRUDENCE

(i) The study, knowledge, science or philosophy of law.
(ii) The legal system, and the theory and practice of law.
(iii) The court and trial system used to administer law and deliver justice, is one example of jurisprudence in action.

LAW

(i) The system of rules which a particular country or community recognizes as regulating the actions of its members and whose government may enforce by the imposition of penalties. (ii) A rule of conduct developed by the government or society over a certain territory. (iii) Law follows certain prescribed procedures, practices and customs in order to monitor and deal with crime, business, social relationships, property, finance, etc.

JURISDICTION

(i) The power and authority to make legal decisions and judgements and the extent and limitations of that power in regards to: (a) position-or-office, (b) territory, (c) the law, and (d) the order of primacy and authority of law.

ORDER OF PRIMACY OF LAW

(A) Four primary sources of *positive* (written) law apply in Ireland. In order of supremacy these are: (i) European Union Law. (ii) The Irish Constitution. (iii) Irish Legislation. (iv) Common Law & Case Law. (B) Secondary forms of law include 'statutory instruments' such as Court Rules etc.

Our primary objective is to provide for 'legal certainty' on matters brought to the PTI for consideration.

SECTION ONE

ETHOS AND GENERAL PRINCIPLES

In respect of the various texts, Reports and publications referred to herein that detail the documented grounds for the establishment of the PTI according to the Rule of Law, it would be redundant to repeat each again in full in this handbook other than to summarise the general principles, ethos & motivations by which the PTI will guide its internal operations.

1. **Professionalism.** Notwithstanding that the PTI has commenced operations with a volunteer staff with limited funding and resources, we nevertheless undertake to conduct PTI operations to the highest professional standards possible.

2. **Lawfulness.** Inasmuch as the PTI Council so determines and controls, PTI operations will be conducted absolutely and explicitly according to the Rule of Law.

3. **Teamwork.** Of necessity, the PTI must have some organisational structure and functional hierarchy. These necessities should not overshadow the collaborative ethos, but should be seen as facilitating the same.

4. **Collaboration.** As per clause (vii) of the PTI Mission Statement, the PTI remains open to collaboration with any individual, agency or association, whether private, corporate or statutory, that has shared objectives.

5. **Openness and Transparency.** With due regard to the law in respect of such matters as; (i) Data Protection, (ii) the Family Courts and/or (iii) 'legal privilege' for example, as well as (iv) operational practicalities, no PTI procedure will be undertaken other than with full transparency.

6. **Promoting the Overriding Objective:** Inasmuch as is possible and practical to do so, PTI operations will align expressly with, 'The Overriding Objective':

"**The overriding objective** - *That court cases be dealt with justly, efficiently and cost-effectively.*" Dealing with a case 'justly' includes (abridged)—(a) acquitting the innocent and convicting the guilty; (b) dealing with the prosecution and the defence fairly; (c) recognising the rights of a claimant/defendant, particularly those under *Article 6 of the European Convention on Human Rights*; (d) respecting the interests of all parties and keeping them informed of the progress of the case; (e) dealing with the case efficiently and expeditiously; (f) ensuring that appropriate information is available to the court; and (g) dealing with the case in ways that take into account—(i) the gravity of the offence alleged, (ii) the complexity of what is in issue, (iii) the severity of the consequences for the claimant / defendant and others affected, and (iv) the needs of other cases. *"These rules are written to be intelligible not just to lawyers but to litigants-in-person also"*.

Lord Woolf (UK) 1996. (SI 1998/3132) UK.

7. **Pursuing Reform.** Notwithstanding the potentially-punitive functions of the Adjudicating and Prosecuting Divisions and the active use of; (i) lawful citizens arrests, (ii) via criminal prosecutions by common informer, and (iii) through the open publication of all PTI activities including PTI Judicial Rulings and Findings; the primary objective remains that of true reform of the Irish justice system; the eradication of endemic criminality within the institutions of the State, most notably in the DPP's Office and in the Courts; and the introduction of a culture of truth and justice vs the prevailing state of corruption and criminality as embedded in the Department of Justice.

SECTION TWO

LAWFUL AUTHORITIES FOR THE PTI

As explained in the respective texts and publications served on the Irish authorities as referenced in this Guide, the core legal authority for PTI operations is the Rule of Law itself. Specifically, that the 'intrinsic vested jurisdiction' of the Rule of Law provides the PTI (and indeed any other party) the lawful right and authority to produce literal and precise *interpretations* of the application of the Rule of Law, especially in circumstances where the Irish State is repeatedly failing the people in this regard. 'The Rule of Law' is not to be confused with the similar-sounding phrases, "*a* rule of law" or mere "rule *by* law" (which is further explained in Section 7) but refers explicitly to *the Rule of Law* (in capitals) which is a universally-recognised set of principles that encompasses fundamental human rights.

THE UNIVERSAL PRINCIPLES
OF THE RULE OF LAW

That the government as well as private actors are accountable under the law. That the laws are clear, publicized, and stable; that they are applied evenly; and that they protect fundamental rights, including the security of persons and contract, of property, and of human rights.

In particular, the PTI will *only* deal with submissions in context of what is known in legal circles as 'positive law'. 'Positive' in this context does not mean 'positive vs negative' *per se*, but refers to the fact that these laws have been 'posited' (or deposited) in writing, meaning literally 'on the record' in written form, which arguably should leave little room for errors or misinterpretation. When coupled with an understanding of the various different *types* of laws and in which order of precedence they should be applied, along with an appreciation of how the jurisdiction of various courts, individual judges or other agencies determine the reach, the limitations and/or the power-and-authority of each particular entity to interpret, apply and/or enforce the law; one arrives at a relatively simple formula under which the Rule of Law can be documented. It is the position of the founders of PTI—and one of the key grounds for the establishment of the PTI in the first place—that many of the serial errors, mistakes, violations and misapplications of the law which emanate out of the Irish Courts could be rectified—at least on paper—by the proper interpretation of the law.

This 'proper interpretation of the law' will be the central pillar upon which PTI operations will be based, and, in making those considered literal interpretations, we will be scrupulous in avoiding convoluted legalese and formal Latin, and will not indulge in any unnecessarily elaborate and tortuous 'legal opinions' which in many cases offer little clarity on the law and seem designed (whether intentionally or otherwise) to complicate and obfuscate matters instead of simply applying the Rule of Law in its most elementary and authoritative form, based *solely and explicitly on written positive law*. To be clear, this is NOT 'practicing law' per se. This is *interpreting* the law. The following 'QTC Notices' outline the general terms under which the PTI claims its lawful authority to do so.

'QTC 1' – NOTICE & CONSTITUTIONAL DECLARATION

This formal NOTICE is hereby presented and served in regards to our fundamental human rights & in support of the constitutional position; that we are indeed guaranteed by inalienable right the confirmed protections of the Irish Constitution and those of the European Union and cannot lawfully be instructed, coerced or directed by any agents of the Irish State to act in contravention of these fundamental doctrines, nor to knowingly engage in unlawful, unconstitutional or criminal activity, and the State is hereby held strictly liable for any such breaches, including for any physical or psychological injuries or distress caused, and for all related costs and expenses.

1. Irish judges ARE subject to the law and the Constitution.

2. Members of the public ARE entitled to a fair hearing in the Irish Courts.

3. Judges of the District Court, Circuit Court and High Court ARE obliged to adhere to Supreme Court rulings, decisions and directions.

4. When any person in the pay of the State commits a criminal offence, they ARE subject to justice in our Courts in the same way as the tax-paying public are.

5. If any given judge deliberately breaks the law, the Constitution, their solemn Oath of Office or any other Act or Statute in the Courtroom; then any such hearing, or any decisions or pronouncements so rendered are, self-evidently, void and invalid.

6. Members of the public are NOT obliged to comply with unlawful, unconstitutional or criminal directions from any statutory authority figure such as a member of An Garda Síochána, by Courts Service staff or by members of the Judiciary.

7. Law-abiding members of the public ARE guaranteed their constitutional safety and will NOT be unlawfully assaulted, injured or incarcerated whilst in the Courtroom.

8. All citizens and residents of this State have the right to issue private criminal proceedings, without cost or hindrance, against ANY other person, citizen or employee of the State under the terms of *The Petty Sessions (Ireland) Act 1851*.

9. Any such application, provided there is *prima facie* evidence of the crime alleged (and failing any extraordinary circumstances) MUST be dealt with on the day.

10. Notwithstanding the above, statutory provisions DO exist for the investigation of—and the removal of—judges of the various Courts for stated, *'incapacity, infirmity, misbehaviour and/or misconduct'* (in general or on specific occasion):

- S. 73 of The Courts of Justice Act 1924
- S. 21 of The Courts of Justice (District Court) Act 1946
- S. 10.1 (iv) of The Courts (Supplemental Provisions) Act, 1961
- S. 9 of The Houses of the Oireachtas (Privileges and Procedures) Act 2013
- Article 35.4 (i) of the Irish Constitution

ENDORSED *'QUI TACET CONSENTIT'* AUGUST 2016
*By: **The President of Ireland**, Michael D. Higgins; **An Taoiseach** Enda Kenny TD; **Minister for Justice & Tánaiste** Frances Fitzgerald TD; **Garda Commissioner** Nóirín O'Sullivan; **Attorney General** Marie Whelan; **Director of Public Prosecutions** Claire Loftus; **Chief Justice** Susan Denham (and any and all State-sponsored affiliates or subordinates thereof).*

'QTC 2' – NOTICE & DECLARATION – May 2019

1. ALL residents and citizens of this State – without exception – are subject to the law and the Constitution.

2. In addition, 'Irish officials' including civil servants, public servants and office holders are bound by their respective Codes of Conduct / Oaths of Office / Customer Charters.

3. Any non-statutory; (i) denials; (ii) inordinate delays; (iii) unqualified refusals; (iv) unexplained failures or departures from; and/or any (v) deliberate, calculated, reckless, negligent or conscious abuses of service due to members of the public, or to other agents or agencies of the State, would constitute a *prima facie* violation of the respective regulations.

4. Where any such violations can be attributed to; (a) dishonest, disingenuous, fraudulent, collusive or malicious actions or intentions on the part of the offender(s) and/or; (b) to discriminatory, prejudicial, unjust or inequitable motives; for the purposes of (c) visiting punitive, detrimental, unlawful or unconstitutional consequences, and/or amercement and personal distress on the persons suffering the said violations; that said violations would constitute *"corrupt"* and/or *"criminal"* acts as defined in the respective *Criminal Justice Acts:*

(i) "corruptly" includes acting with an improper purpose personally or by influencing another person whether – (a) by means of making a false or misleading statement; (b) by means of withholding, concealing, altering or destroying a document or other information, or; (c) by other means.

(ii) a crime or offence (or criminal offence) is an act

harmful not only to some individual but also to a community, society or the state ("a public wrong").

5. When any such violations are committed in context of; (i) the offender's potential advancement in their statutory/ official role; (ii) for their own or another's personal benefit; and/or (iii) in *de facto* expectation of the same; that such would constitute a *"consideration"* or *"advantage"* as defined in *the Criminal Justice (Corruption Offences) Act 2018, & EU law.*

6. When and where any such violations are knowingly committed in context of legal proceedings, that such would also constitute 'offences against the administration of justice'.

7. That any knowing compliance, assistance or facilitation of any such improper or unlawful acts by any other person would constitute direct complicity with any such unlawful acts.

8. That as per the respective Irish and EU legislation, it remains unlawful for any resident or citizen of this State to knowingly participate in unlawful, corrupt or criminal activities.

As endorsed April-May 2019 by the Offices of: (i) The President of Ireland; (ii) The Taoiseach; (iii) The Chief Justice; (iv) The Attorney General; (v) The Minister for Justice; (vi) The DPP; (vii) The CSSO.

IRISH CONSTITUTION, ARTICLE 40.1.

"All citizens shall, as human persons, be held equal before the law."

STATEMENT & DECLARATION
('QTC 3' – March 2020)

This document acquired force of law *'qui tacet consentit videtur' (silence implies consent)* March 9th 2020

1. Natural law (or moral law) is unwritten law that defines what is fundamentally 'right and wrong'.

2. Positive law is written law which defines what is 'legal or illegal' at any given time, in any place.

3. Four primary sources of *positive* (vs. natural) law apply in Ireland. In order of supremacy these are: (i) European Union Law. (ii) The Irish Constitution. (iii) Irish Legislation. (iv) Common Law & Case Law.

4. Secondary sources of positive law are known as 'statutory instruments' including; (a) ministerial orders, (b) governmental regulations, (c) operational rules, and (d) bye-laws (for example). These are delegated to regulatory bodies and local authorities. But they **must** be consistent with, and based on, the legislation adopted by the Oireachtas; otherwise they can be challenged in the Courts.

5. To contravene the law by any act or omission is to commit an unlawful, illicit and/or criminal act. "Lawbreaking" is also variously defined as; *'crime, breach, malefaction, misbehaviour, misconduct, misdeed, misfeasance, malfeasance, nonfeasance, transgression, trespass, violation & wrongdoing.'*

6. Accordingly, any person who, with full knowledge, awareness and understanding of the same, deliberately and knowingly: (i) disregards, (ii) ignores, (iii) defies; (iv) disobeys; (v) contravenes, (vi) breaches, (vii) flouts, or (viii) violates any such primary or secondary source of

law is—by virtue of the said illicit act or omission—committing a *prima facie* offence against the said law and is subject to the criminal penalties and/or legal consequences, if any, that apply in those circumstances.

7. Any such offending person including any Irish officials or office holders who engage in lawbreaking either; (a) in their private capacity as residents or citizens; and/or (b) in context of their public role or position, are subject to the respective legal consequences by way of: (i) criminal complaints to An Garda Siochána, and/or (ii) prosecution by the DPP; and/or (iii) by way of private, criminal prosecution under *S.10 of the Petty Sessions (Ireland) Act 1851*, and/or (iv) are also subject to legitimate citizen's arrest as per the terms of *S.4 of the Criminal Law Act 1997* & *S.12 of the Criminal Damage Act 1991*.

8. In particular, any Irish judge who, with full knowledge, awareness and understanding of the same, deliberately and knowingly: (i) disregards, (ii) ignores, (iii) defies; (iv) disobeys; (v) contravenes, (vi) breaches, (vii) flouts, or (viii) violates any such *primary* source of law whilst engaged in their role as judge is—by virtue of the said illicit act or omission—in added violation of: (a) *the Universal Declaration of Human Rights*; (b) *The International Covenant on Civil and Political Rights*; (c) *The United Nations Basic Principles on the Independence of the Judiciary*; (d) *The Council of Europe's European Charter on the Statute for Judges*; (e) *The European Convention on Human Rights* (ECHR); and (f) *The (UN Drafted) Bangalore Principles of Judicial Conduct*—and any such offending judge is therefore committing a *prima facie* criminal offence as against the administration of justice, which in turn would constitute literal 'judicial misbehaviour' as per the terms of *Article 35.4(i) of the Irish Constitution*, which said 'misbehaviour' is grounds

for impeachment and removal from office.

9. "Incapacity" is the second criteria under which a judge may be removed from office. Accordingly, should it be demonstrated that any given judge is physically, mentally or psychologically 'incapable' – or indeed has been rendered incapable of lawfully conducting his office through personal, moral, ethical, political or financial compromises, that any such judge should be removed from office.

10. Where proofs or supported allegations of judicial misbehaviour or incapacity are formally made known to any Member of Dáil Éireann or Seanad Éireann, the Constitution requires that the said person(s) refer the matter to the Government as per the terms of *Article 35.4(i) of the Constitution.*

IRISH CONSTITUTION, ARTICLE 40.3.

"1° The State guarantees in its laws to respect, and, as far as practicable, by its laws to defend and vindicate the personal rights of the citizen.

2° The State shall, in particular, by its laws protect as best it may from unjust attack and, in the case of injustice done, vindicate the life, person, good name, and property rights of every citizen."

The European Court of Justice uses 6 criteria to qualify 'a competent domestic tribunal'. These are fully discussed in Section Seven of this Handbook.

In addition to the three previous 'QTC' Notices, 'QTC 4' at the rear of this Handbook was also served on the authorities in June 2020 and which said document makes clear reference to other pertinent texts including the Declaration at Section 7 and to the published book: *"Criminality in the Irish Courts and the absence of the Rule of Law"* which contains a detailed listing of many EU and domestic laws, the persistent violations of which have created the legal, moral, constitutional and jurisdictional void that will now be filled by the Peoples Tribunal so as not to jeopardise Ireland's continued membership of the UN, the CoE and the EU. For the sake of clarity however, other primary legal principles upon which the authority of the PTI is established; to interpret positive law and issue formal findings & Rulings includes:

- The right of access to justice
- The right to fair procedures
- The right to a fair trial
- The right to a fair hearing
- The right to equality of arms
- The right to access a lawyer
- The right to adversarial proceedings
- The right to a reasoned decision
- The right to be informed of proceedings
- The right to the independence and impartiality of 'tribunals' (courts)
- The right to legal aid in criminal proceedings
- The right to be advised, defended and *effectively* represented in criminal proceedings
- The right to accuracy of the record
- The right *not* to be subjected to 'excessive formalism'

- The right to adequate time and facilities to prepare
- The right of access to the case file
- The right to legal aid in appeal hearings
- The right to an effective remedy
- The right to a presumption of innocence
- The right of the court to overrule or overturn a decision by the DPP to prosecute
- The right to a genuine, authentic appeal system
- The right to be compensated upon proof of criminal wrongdoing by the State

..and upon these aspects of positive, written law.

- *THE UNIVERSAL DECLARATION OF HUMAN RIGHTS (UDHR) – 1948*
- *THE EUROPEAN CONVENTION ON HUMAN RIGHTS (ECHR) i.e. The Convention for the Protection of Human Rights and Fundamental Freedoms - 1953*
- *THE INTERNATIONAL COVENANT ON CIVIL AND POLITICAL RIGHTS (ICCPR) - 1966*
- *THE UNITED NATIONS BASIC PRINCIPLES ON THE INDEPENDENCE OF THE JUDICIARY - 1985*
- *THE COUNCIL OF EUROPE'S EUROPEAN CHARTER ON THE STATUTE FOR JUDGES - 1998*
- *THE (UN DRAFTED) BANGALORE PRINCIPLES OF JUDICIAL CONDUCT (OHCHR) – 2003*
- *THE EUROPEAN CONVENTION ON HUMAN RIGHTS ACT 2003 (ECHR ACT)*

And finally, the simple fact that on the evidence produced and other than sporadically, in random Courts and by occasional judges, that there is in fact NO legitimate, consistent 'competent domestic tribunal' that operates specifically and expressly under the Rule of Law in this State other than the Peoples Tribunal of Ireland.

SECTION THREE

GENERAL STRUCTURE AND FORMATION

The PTI will take the following centralised form, as directed by the Executive, until such time as an elected PTI Council votes upon a different format. Any such altered format should align with; (i) the PTI Mission Statement; (ii) the Ethos and Principles of the PTI; and (iii) in particular with the concept of the Overriding Principle as laid out in Section One, Article 6.

1. There will be a permanent listed address for the receipt of correspondence and to serve as a central office with whatever facilities and amenities the PTI Council deems necessary to fulfil the status of a 'permanent competent domestic tribunal' as per EU regulations.

2. The main responsibilities of running the PTI will be shared amongst the 13-person Council to include a 3-person Executive (Chairperson, Secretary and Treasurer) operating in a collaborative shared role, plus 40 named Operations Officers to include one Data Controller who will also serve as Aide to the Executive. This volunteer corps of 53 persons will be known collectively as, "the PTI Administration" ('PTI Admin') who will each have voting rights at the next AGM according to PTI Rules.

3. All other persons who declare an interest in the PTI and who have filled out the basic membership form will be known collectively as 'the PTI Panel'. There will be no other limits or restrictions on such PTI Panel membership other than proof of I.D. and the signed disclaimer on the application form. These persons may contribute in many constructive ways to the operations, functions and processes of the PTI as laid out in Section Four.

4. Other parties who wish to contribute to PTI operations are of course free to do so, whether or not they have signed up to the PTI Panel. 'Contributions' so described may include personal or professional advice or opinions that are delivered via emails, phone calls or other mediums for example, including raising questions or posting commentary on the PTI website(s)*. Any such contributions from recognised individuals or institutions will be credited back to that source except in circumstances where that source has requested anonymity. *(*To include affiliated media platforms).*

5. The PTI also welcomes contributions from anonymous sources. These must be assessed on their merits and tested for credibility before they can be applied to PTI matters. If verification is difficult or time-consuming, then such contributions may need to be filed, unused.

6. With particular respect to the pandemic-related social restrictions and the advantages of online technology, the 'PTI Admin' may operate remotely or in chosen locations as the circumstances require.

7. The 1st PTI Executive are the founders of the PTI. The remaining members of the 1st PTI Council will be directly appointed by the Executive during the initiating 12-month operational phase. Each Councillor may, in turn, appoint up to 3 Operations Officers. The Executive will select the Data Controller. This arrangement will remain in place until c. July 1st 2021 whereupon all new Council positions will be filled by PTI Admin ballot at the AGM.

8. The PTI Admin will operate in 3 Divisions: (i) Investigations; (ii) Adjudications; (iii) Prosecutions.

9. Councillors will be expected to assume shared responsibility for one of the 3 Divisions. Where possible, one member of the Executive will guide each Division.

Anticipated Assignment of Responsibilities

Investigations Division

Accepting and assessing all submissions (by topic, case and/or issue) and evaluating the evidence / researching the law / liaising with parties and preparing files for consideration by the Council.

1 Executive + 3 Councillors + 13 Operations Officers

Adjudicating Division

Holding private sittings or public hearings as mediators, arbitrators, adjudicators, judges, and issuing subpoenas, rulings, findings, judgments, decisions and mandates strictly according to law.

1 Executive + 2 Councillors + 13 Operations Officers

Prosecutions Division

Preparing cases for criminal prosecution 'in the public interest' in the domestic law courts under *The Petty Sessions Act* and providing for citizen's arrests under *S.4 of the Criminal Law Act 1997.*

1 Executive + 5 Councillors + 13 Operations Officers

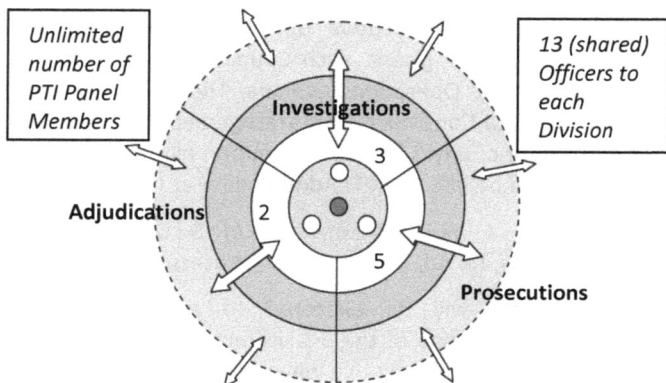

PTI Council = 13 Councillors (3 Executive)

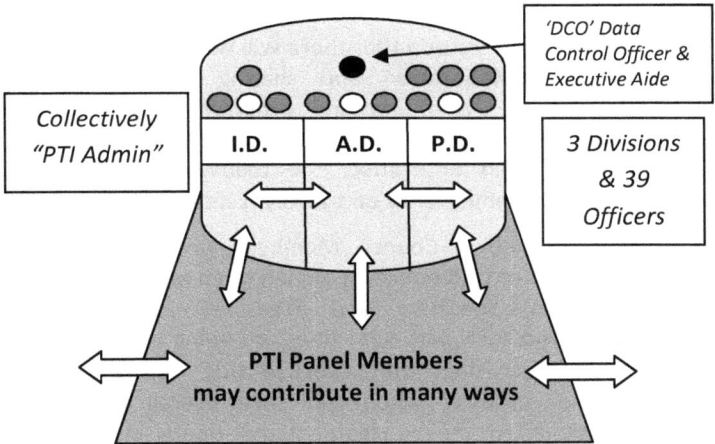

'DCO' Data Control Officer & Executive Aide

Collectively "PTI Admin"

I.D.   A.D.   P.D.

3 Divisions & 39 Officers

PTI Panel Members may contribute in many ways

10. **"THE PTI ADMINISTRATION"** comprises the PTI Executive (3 persons) plus 10 more Council Members and 40 Operations Officers, one of whom is the Data Protection Officer and Aide to the Executive.

11. **"The PTI Council"** comprises the Executive + 10 Council Members through whom all final decisions will be made.

12. **There are three Divisions:** (i) Investigations ('I.D.') (ii) Adjudications ('A.D.') (iii) Prosecutions ('P.D.') – each guided by Councillors, assisted by Operations Officers.

13 **"Operations Officers" (OO)** comprise existing, proven pro-justice activists and enthusiasts who have something of direct value to offer to the PTI. Each Councillor can nominate up to 3 Officers to assist in any Division or area of operation as required = max 53 PTI Officials total (including the Council and the Aide to the Executive). The Council may fill any 'OO' vacancies as they arise or occur.

Key Roles and Responsibilities

Whilst it is understood that there will be a great deal of necessary collaboration and sharing of time and resources as PTI operations progress and evolve, including the likelihood that the staffing of operations will be a fluid enterprise, the following guidelines should offer some clarity on the key roles of the PTI.

The Executive: 3 Council Members who share the responsibilities traditionally assigned to an organisation's Chairperson, Secretary and Treasurer respectively. However, no such particular titles are being assigned at the PTI other than the collective title of, "The PTI Executive" each of whom will take overall (shared) responsibility for the management and supervision of the respective PTI Divisions in line with PTI objectives.

Councillors: 10 additional Council Members who will assign themselves to Divisions according to interest and capability. The 13-person Council has final say on all PTI-related matters – as duly considered at QM's and AGM's.

Operations Officers ('OO'): Invited and appointed by Councillors to assist in PTI operations. OO's have voting and speaking rights at the AGM where the new Council is elected. They may also be invited to contribute at Council meetings on prior Notice to, from or by the Executive.

Data Control Officer ('DCO'): Required by new legislation to ensure compliance with GDPR etc. The DCO will have the same voting and speaking rights as the 'OO's and functions as the Aide to the Executive, working with the three Divisions to prepare the agendas for QM's, SCM's and at the AGM.

Investigating Division: This is the primary, sole (official) entry point for all correspondence, information, applications and submissions to PTI. The I.D.'s main responsibility is to field, sort and qualify incoming correspondence and information with a view to putting matters before the Council at the next formal meeting. The I.D. will also liaise with the *mycasehistory* website for the purposes of setting up new accounts for those making Case Submissions. The I.D.'s other important functions are to correspond with those submitters, to pursue relevant information and secure evidence, to do research, and compile data that will assist the PTI Council in achieving its goals and objectives. It should be noted however, that much of the responsibility to provide materials rests *solely* on those making Case Submissions.

Adjudicating Division: Receives case files and/or General Submissions from the Council (and *only* from the Council) and sets about the process of; (i) assigning the matter for arbitration or mediation, and/or; (ii) resolving and/or adjudicating on the matter strictly according to written, positive law, either by written rulings with-or-without formal sittings or hearings, as the case may be. Findings or decisions are then returned to the Council for majority approval before being endorsed and made public.

Prosecutions Division: Acts *only* with the majority approval of the Council on matters that have been fully processed by the PTI. The P.D. can; (i) initiate criminal prosecutions in the name of the Irish People in the domestic Courts; (ii) may direct and conduct lawful citizens' arrests; and/or (iii) may act in lawful support of PTI Members who are before the domestic Courts.

Administrator for the PTI Website: The primary online platform for all PTI-related matters and documentation.

Manager of the Case Submissions website: This is a separate, privately-owned operation that provides web pages at *mycasehistory.com* (the 'MCH website') to those making Case Submissions, the operation and management of which must remain completely independent, given that its services are open to the general public and given the webmaster's obligation to police potentially-unlawful materials.

Public Relations and Media Interface: Because the PTI operates on the principle of shared responsibility, no single individual or group of individuals within the PTI Admin may address the media on PTI-related topics without the express permission of the Council using an authorised prepared statement.

The only other forms of interview that may be given to the mainstream media will be in the following formats:

- At a general or specific formal media conference where a majority of the Council is represented including at least 2 members of the Executive.
- By way of publication of PTI findings, rulings, reports or judgments as authorised by Council.
- By way of formal press releases as endorsed by Council.

Membership & Recruitment: It is the responsibility of all Councillors to promote the work and objectives of the PTI and to actively recruit persons who would be suitable to serve on the PTI Panel and/or be elected to Council.

Other Roles & Responsibilities: These may be assigned or created by the Executive or by the Council as required to compliment the work of the respective Divisions – especially in the initiating phase. In certain cases, such as the recruitment of additional ad-hoc investigators adjudicators or prosecutors in special cases for example, the Executive may assign temporary roles as 'PTI Admin' to any such persons, for limited periods.

SECTION FOUR

PROCESSES & PROCEEDURES

It is fundamental to the efficient operation of the PTI that all PTI Admin personnel adhere to these basic guidelines and procedures which may be amended or updated by majority Council vote, as per PTI Rules.

1. All correspondence to the PTI *must* be fielded through the Investigations Division. There can be no exceptions to this rule. The I.D. will have authority to view all submissions and correspondence to the PTI unless such action is deemed unlawful, or proscribed in the PTI Rules.

2. If any party wishes to communicate 'privately' with any PTI Admin on any PTI-related matters, said matters cannot be raised at Council other than by folllowing the relevant procedures as laid out hereunder – by Motion to the Council via the I.D. or directly through the DCO.

3. Other than routine administrative business, all matters for official consideration by the Executive must also come via the I.D. and from there to the DCO. Such correspondence may be delivered unopened to the DCO, but the existence of that correspondence should be on the agenda for the next Quarterly Meeting (QM), any Special Council Meeting (SCM) or the Annual General Meeting (AGM) whichever comes first.

4. All formal correspondence sent to the Executive will be made known to the Council either by summary or by a full reading thereof *before* any response issues. Any such response may only issue in the name of the Council and with the majority approval of Council. No formal correspondence shall be carried over unread at any QM, SCM or AGM.

5. Four Quarterly Meetings will be held on-or-around the beginning of July, October, January and April as laid out in Section Five. Except in cases where a Special Council Meeting (SCM) or Emergency General Meeting (EGM) has been called to address a specific matter, the QM is the sole forum for Council to decide on PTI matters and operations. The AGM may incorporate a QM or SCM.

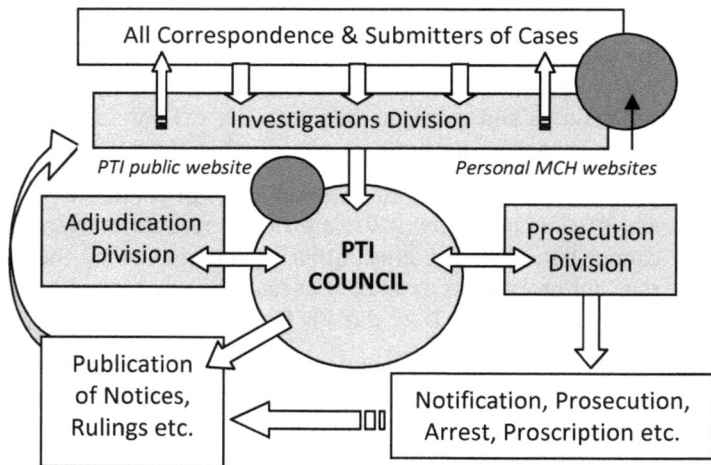

6. The Investigations Division's responsibilities include:

- The receipt and processing of *all* incoming correspondence of any type.
- The assessment of submissions and their preparation for forwarding to the PTI Council for consideration.
- Conducting any necessary communication with submitters as to the status of their submission.
- Liaising with www.mycasehistory.com for the purposes of documenting case stories.
- Actively conducting general research and

investigations into any relevant matters.
- The maintenance of a general PTI database and filing system for the service of the Council.

7. The Adjudication Division's responsibilities will include:
- Receiving submissions from the Council.
- Processing those submissions according to type and setting a schedule for meetings, hearings and/or judicial sittings as the case may be.
- Issuing interim Notices, Advisories, Subpoenas and Judgments as-and-when required.
- Returning to the Council with their findings and conclusions according to written, positive law.
- Actively recruiting suitably experienced or qualified persons to serve as adjudicators, arbitrators, mediators, counsellors and judges.

8. The Prosecutions Division's responsibilities include:
- Receiving information, documentation and instructions from the Council that identifies criminal offences by named individuals.
- Initiating proceedings against named persons under the respective legislation to include; (a) the lodging of formal criminal complaints with An Garda Siochána, and/or (b) the initiation of criminal proceedings in the domestic Courts.
- Providing for the lawful citizen's arrest of persons accused of proven criminal offences.
- Selecting, training and appointing PTI Panel members for P.D.-related tasks and operations.

SUBMISSIONS – Types & Criteria

9. Submissions to the PTI will take one of two formats, either, (i) a General Submission, or (ii) a Case Submission.

(i) **General Submissions** ('GS') may arrive in any format in the form of a specific question, a letter or an email, which raises an important topic or issue, or, via a news article for example. The I.D. will field any such General Submissions and where appropriate will list them on the agenda for Council discussion at the next QM.

(ii) **Case Submissions** ('CS') may *only* be accepted on the standard CS Form, complete with fee and personal I.D. The Investigations Division will then process the CS according to the procedure laid out at Articles 41 – 57.

10. It is critical to PTI operations that we only bring matters forwards to Council that are evidence-based, with the respective proofs having been qualified by the I.D. beforehand. All named parties to the case must be identifiable. The PTI cannot and will not be dealing with allegations, claims, stories or unfounded opinions or hearsay from any source unless such is presented in the form of a sworn affidavit, where the submitter clearly understands the consequences of committing perjury.

11. Submissions to the PTI should be 'timed' by the submitting party to arrive not less than 14 days before the next scheduled QM. Those that arrive less than 14 days before may be carried over to the following QM.

12. All Submissions to the PTI will be assigned a Reference Number by; (a) submission type, (b) month, (c) year, (d) sequence and (e) by a Councillor's initials. The 'type' will be either 'GS' or 'CS' (General, or Case Submission) and the Councillor's initials will be those of the Councillor who makes the initial decision either; (i) to sponsor, or (ii) to reject the submission. For example: "PTI-GS-08-2020-001-STM". This number is then noted on the respective Submission Cover Form and travels with the submission until such time as it is filed away.

13. The Submission Cover Form will track the progress of any submission from first receipt or proposal, and the

details of any administrative decisions pertaining to it.

14. OO's (Operations Officers) may act as proposers and/or as submitters of any case or matter that comes to their attention, and may present the same to the I.D. for a reference number. But any such matter cannot be brought to Council without sponsorship by a Councillor.

15. 'Sponsorship' means solely that a Councillor has verified that the submission qualifies to be sent to Council. Submissions will then be assigned to any appropriate Division and to any volunteer for processing.

16. For the sake of expediency, General Submissions which are clearly vexatious or nonsensical need not be assigned PTI reference numbers before being briefly discussed at Council. The decision to reject or discard that topic / issue / question should however be noted in the PTI Rejections File for future reference and to avoid repeat rejections and wasted administration time.

17. General Submissions concerning matters which, in the opinion of Council, may be beyond the scope or logistical ability of the PTI to deal with at that time will be carried over to the next QM with the SCF duly updated.

18. Submissions may be made to the I.D. at anytime. These will be listed according to the order they were received and, as-and-when they qualify, will be presented to Council in that same chronological order.

19. There will be two types of decision regarding the processing of GS's and CS's. (a) Interim decisions, and (b) final decisions. All such decisions will be tracked on the SCF and inasmuch as any submission remains 'live' its status will be raised at the QM and updated accordingly.

20. Only *final* decisions or final Rulings of Council are open to appeal, and any such appeal will be treated as a

case resubmission. *(See 'Appeals' on page 46)*

21. **Case Submissions** *must* meet two criteria before they will be considered by the I.D. (i) The identity of the submitter must be established, and (ii) the processing fee is paid. No CS will be accepted, processed or discussed by the PTI unless and until it meets these two criteria.

22. Case Submissions that meet those two criteria are immediately; (i) assigned a CS PTI Reference Number and (ii) a Submissions Cover Form (SCF). (iii) The case is then listed on the PTI Submissions Log, and (iv) notification and payment is sent to the *mycasehistory.com* website for the setting up of the submitter's case profile.

23. The I.D. then examines the CS to determine if the matter can come before the Council, and may liaise with the submitter as required or necessary to qualify the CS.

24. If the I.D. finds that the CS does *not* meet the criteria to be sent forwards to Council then the submitter is advised accordingly, with a view to the submitter using the *mycasehistory* online facility to update their case story with whatever particulars or evidence that may be required to bring the case to Council *before* the next QM.

25. If the submitter can amend / correct / provide as required by the I.D. *within the required timeframe* (i.e. *before* the next QM) then the CS will attract a SC sponsor and the matter can be brought to Council.

26. If the submitter does not respond as required, then the CS will be filed as 'incomplete' pending an updated submission of the same case at a future date, which will attract a modest resubmission fee of not more than 20%.

27. Submissions that are deemed 'too complex' by the I.D. or by the Council will attract an advisory to the submitter to resubmit certain portions of their case as

separate submissions. *(See details at Articles 41-57)*.

28. Submissions that are deemed to be 'non-processable' for any other reason should have that reason recorded on the SCF and the submitter advised accordingly.

29. Each resubmitted issue will carry the original PTI CS reference number with each respective portion numbered in succession in brackets, plus the date of resubmission, and any other required information.

30. All new submissions, whether sponsored, rejected or placed 'on hold' must be raised at Council at the next QM, where the respective Councillors should qualify their various decisions in person – or by proxy.

31. Any submission may have its status changed by majority vote of the Council.

32. Sponsored submissions must attract a majority vote of the Council before being forwarded to the Adjudicating Division or to the Prosecutions Division for actioning.

33. All official papers that issue out of the PTI (such as rulings, findings, judgments, summonses, mandates, subpoenas, directives etc) will bear the print-stamp of the respective Division and the internally-identifiable signatures (or initials) of at least 3 Councillors.

34. Final documents that have fully processed through the Adjudications Division and endorsed by Council may be collectively and generically referred to as 'PTI Rulings'.

35. The PTI Seal will remain in the possession of the DCO and can only be used by the Executive, in consultation with the Council and with majority Council approval.

36. Other than GS's and CS's, any other matter that is to be raised at Council that requires any alterations or

amendments to PTI protocols or procedures as outlined in this Handbook must be presented on a PTI Motion Form and endorsed by at least 3 Councillors in advance of being raised at Council. In certain circumstances the requirement for a Motion in advance of the meeting may be waived on condition that the Motion is drawn up by the respective endorsing Councillors immediately following the meeting, such document to be approved by the Executive and then placed 'on file' without delay.

37. The lead Councillor in each Division may adopt whatever procedures, forms or processes deemed to be necessary to provide efficient service as long as this does not conflict with the PTI Ethos / Mission Statement and/or Rules as laid out herein.

38. All documents or submissions that are provided or returned to Council for a decision and/or for publication etc., must be stamped with the relevant Divisional Stamp and signed by the lead Councillor of that Division (or by their proxy). The presence of that Stamp informs the Council that the Division has completed their particular tasks and processes.

39. The Council may decide at any time by majority vote to publish all, or part of, any aspect of any submission before the PTI. Any such publication will be made public on the website as well as in the annual PTI Report. Before publication or release, the original document will be stamped and embossed and filed in the PTI archive. Where necessary or required, up to 2 additional copies of that original document may be embossed for legal purposes, such as endorsing an authority to prosecute or arrest for example, where the original must remain filed.

40. All such published documents will be copyrighted to the PTI but are otherwise free and available to any and

all persons, agencies or institutions for their own independent use provided the original format and contents of the said PTI documents are reproduced in whole, complete as originals, and devoid of alterations.

Case Submissions (CS) – Criteria & Protocols

41. Amongst the most debilitating aspects of administrative processes are; (i) lack of proper planning, organisation and direction, and (ii) allowing unnecessarily complicated bureaucratic procedures to evolve and develop. The result is a morass of chaotic and repetitive paperwork and time-wasting individual arguments about the internal rules and processes, which then have to be resolved through additional bureaucratic processes, etc. Meanwhile, the Overriding Objective is often lost and forgotten. The experts advise us that the best and most efficient way to avoid the typical frustrations we usually associate with officialdom is when an organisation is:

"..open and clear about policies and procedures and ensuring that information, and any advice provided, is clear, accurate and complete. Stating its criteria for decision making and giving reasons for decisions. Handling information properly and appropriately. Keeping proper and appropriate records."

42. Accordingly, and in recognition of the fact that most people's cases are almost always a complex mix of overlapping elements and issues, be it thematic, logistical, law-related, chronological, topical or relating to particular individuals or agencies with aspects that cross-over in myriad ways with various other parts of their respective stories; then, in order not to descend into a morass of chaos upon receipt of each new case submission which will invariably be presented in the submitter's own unique language and opinions which

then has to be studied and understood by all parties involved; instead, the PTI has prepared a relatively simple classification system by which each submitter can identify in advance what particular type of submission they are making. This will help streamline and simplify the process for all parties involved, whilst at the same time providing for an easily-referenced PTI database of cases, issues and outcomes that will be available to all.

43. The PTI Case Submission Form is designed to facilitate this process, but it will be helpful to all users of the PTI to have a general understanding of how the system will—and indeed must—work, if we are to make any real progress with individual cases, topics and issues.

44. Firstly, the prospective submitter should contact the PTI to advise that they wish to make a submission. It is highly advisable that the submitter pays the submission fee at this point because they will have immediate access to their own MCH webpage which MCH facility is central to the efficient processing of case submissions.

45. The submitter will then be directed to the instructions on the PTI website, where they will find the case-type classifications, which are based on common wrongs / injuries / offences that have been reported to the PTI. *(Space is provided for new/uncategorised issues).*

46. The submitter then identifies whichever of these issues they are asking the PTI to make a Ruling on, and lists them on their submission paperwork, along with the chronology of their general over-story (meaning the narrative that gives overall context to the specific listed issue) – which will also be on their MCH webpage. This 'general over-story' therefore, may or may not include several discrete 'issues' that are listed for consideration (and of course some identifiable issues may *not* be listed

for consideration by the submitter) **but it is crucial that everybody understands that the PTI is set up to deal with individual, discrete issues one-at-a-time, in chronological order and in sequence <u>as requested by the submitter</u>**, and NOT with a jumble of interconnected or overlapping issues or events whatever their relationship might be in the general over-story, simply because to attempt to do this would render PTI administration and operations practically unmanageable.

47. Some issues *may* be combined as a practical measure by the PTI, such as if numerous persons have committed the exact same offence for example and the submitter wants individual rulings on all of those persons – in which case, one Ruling could issue that lists all of the individuals' names. Another example might be where two or more offences occur during one particular incident where it is relatively easy to combine the findings of the Adjudicating Division into one Ruling document. But these are internal decisions that will only affect the submitter inasmuch as they may attract secondary resubmission fees or further requests for evidence etc.

48. To reiterate; a person's over-story in their original case submission (and on the *mycasehistory* website) may contain any number of identifiable offences or wrongs, but other than in general commentary in the text of any final Rulings, the PTI will NOT specifically examine any particular 'issue' that has not been; (i) identified in advance, and (ii) specifically requested by the submitter, except in cases where Council decides otherwise in the common good. In any such latter case, there would of course be no resubmission fee to the original submitter.

49. Once the submitter has started their chronology on the *mycasehistory* website, then the PTI can continuously

reference that chronology/over-story and all of the associated evidence as the PTI progresses through each discrete issue that the submitter has listed for consideration on their original Case Submission Form.

50. One of the main tasks for the I.D. therefore will be the identification and separation of the discrete issues listed in each submitter's original CS Form, and then advising the submitter that *only* the first such issue (or combination of issues as decided by the I.D.) will be covered by the original submission fee, and that each of the subsequent issues will attract the standard resubmission fee of not more than 20% before they are brought to Council, provided that each such discrete issue (or collection of combined issues) is resubmitted within 12 months of the issuance of the said PTI advisory.

51. In this manner, both the submitter and the PTI begin to catalogue the individual issues; (i) as discrete entities that have been ruled on by the PTI, and (ii) as components in the overall chronology of the submitter's case, which can then be 'stacked' by the submitter in specific support of key elements of their own over-story.

52. In cases where a submitter already has their case story on the MCH website independently and *before* coming to the PTI, the case submission fee will be 50%.

53. If any submitter wants the PTI to review any *new* incidents that arise *after* the date of their original case submission, then; (i) because these are new submissions that will require a fresh review by the I.D., but also (ii) because the details of any new incidents can simply be added to the submitter's existing chronology on the MCH website, then any such new/additional submissions will only attract a 50% fee.

54. So, to summarise. The best way for any party to make

a case submission would be to decide in the first instance whether; (a) their case contains just one clearly-defined issue that can be ruled on by the PTI, or (b) if their case comprises a sequence of issues that will need to be separated for individual consideration by the PTI.

55. In the case of (a) the procedure is simple. The submitter pays the fee, gets assigned a *mycasehistory* webpage, puts their chronology and evidence up online, submits the CSF, and waits for their case to come before Council.

56. In the case of (b) the submitter follows the same procedure only with the understanding that after they have submitted their CSF, there will be an extra step in the process where the I.D. will help the submitter to identify and separate the various discrete issues for individual consideration by the PTI.

57. It should be clear however, that the *mycasehistory* website has made its facilities available to PTI Members at a discount, so the best (and least expensive) way to avail of both the PTI service and a personal MCH webpage is to come through the PTI case submissions process in the order: (i) Pay fee. (ii) Populate the webpage with chronology and evidence. (iii) Submit CSF.

"It is crucial that everybody understands that the PTI is set up to deal with individual, discrete issues one-at-a-time, in chronological order and in sequence as requested by the submitter, and NOT with a jumble of interconnected or overlapping issues or events whatever their relationship might be in the general over-story; simply because to attempt to do this would render PTI administration and operations practically unmanageable."

CASE SUBMISSION PROCEEDURE

In this example, the chronology (the over-story) spans 3 years from the beginning to the point of approach to the PTI. The submitter can identify 7 clear, separate incidents where they have been wronged, but only want the PTI to review 4 of them (for whatever reasons). So, although the chronology will tell the whole over-story, the submitter needs *only* provide the evidence to support those 4 actionable aspects. In time, the submitter can place as many additional materials as they like to compliment the general over-story online – which will be helpful to anyone viewing the webpage. In this manner, we create both a public record of the member's story as well as an easily-accessed research facility with all of the evidence needed to investigate those 4 particular issues.

Start of case over-story

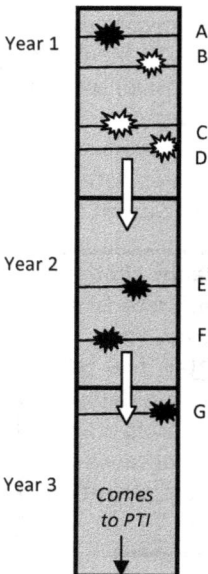

Year 1

A
B

C
D

Year 2

E

F

G

Year 3

Comes to PTI

E.g. This sample story begins with incident 'A' – an assault on the submitter. He reports the matter 'B' to the Guards, but nothing is done. Then 'C' he goes to GSOC, and 'F' files a complaint with Garda HQ. Still nothing! So, 'E' he takes a private action in the Court, but because his attacker is 'politically connected' the Court keeps ruling against him. At 'F' his appeal against those unjust decisions is improperly shut down. Then at 'G' he is arrested on false charges in a clear act of intimidation. He then applies to the PTI to make lawful Rulings on incidents 'A, E, F & G' – and uses those rulings to endorse the over-story; to further his case; and take further action against those who have wronged him...

SECTION FIVE

MEETINGS, HEARINGS, SITTINGS & APPEALS

It is essential that all PTI 'business' is open and transparent and that all major decisions are undertaken only and exclusively by majority vote of the elected Council. This will ensure collective accountability and help promote clear and effective teamwork with common goals. This will also prevent potential individual errors and reduce the PTI's exposure to criticism or attack.

Because of the requirement for Council approval of all major decisions, PTI operations will effectively 'revolve around' scheduled Council meetings, where all valid submissions will be considered, assessed and processed and where existing submissions' status will be reviewed. Persons making submissions or other approaches to the PTI Council should therefore keep this in mind and apply to the I.D. properly prepared and in sufficient time to avoid their submission being held-up, carried-over or rejected which *may* in turn attract a resubmission fee.

MEETINGS – THE AGM

1. An annual AGM will be held on-or-around July 1st each year. All PTI Panel Members are eligible to attend, but only PTI Admin will have speaking and voting rights. The main purpose for this meeting will be to elect the new PTI Council. The date and location of the AGM will be publicised a minimum of 30 days in advance.

2. All PTI Admin personnel are eligible to volunteer for a position on the Council and vote for same. Nominations must be in writing and 14 days or more before the AGM.

3. Additional prospects may be nominated by any Councillor in writing and delivered to the Executive no less than 14 days before the AGM. Council will be duly notified. If 7 or more Councillors subsequently formally object to any given nomination up to 24 hours before the vote, that nomination will be considered withdrawn.

4. The election of the new Council will be the first order of business with the incoming Executive chairing the AGM, with assistance from the outgoing Council as appropriate.

5. Votes will be collected on location according to the procedures determined by the Executive.

6. Accommodation may be made for a separate public meeting or for any other PTI-related function deemed appropriate or necessary by the Council.

QUARTERLY MEETINGS (QM'S) and SCM'S

7. There will be a minimum of four Quarterly Meetings. The basic agenda for each meeting will be arranged by the DCO in consultation with the three operational Divisions. The agenda should be approved by the Executive in advance of meetings, and, as with the AGM, provision may be made for other PTI-related events.

8. The Executive may call a **Special Council Meeting** at any time and/or may hold a 'virtual' meeting if such is the only viable way to gather the Council's opinion on an important matter. No case-related decisions will be made in isolation or in private, by the Executive or by other Councillors without open discussion and a transparent vote at a formal meeting – whether virtual or otherwise.

9. With exception to any part of a QM, SCM or an AGM that is specifically set aside for debate, formal Council meetings will follow the prescribed agenda.

10. Following the initial vetting process by the I.D., any and all subsequent decisions as to the admissibility, viability, progress or conclusion of any submission, may *only* be taken by the Council who will rate and assess each case objectively on its merits, on its overall complexity, and considering the PTI resources available.

11. Any Councillor at any time may call a limited meeting with selected PTI Admin Members to discuss any aspect of PTI Operations or for training or consultation or as is required for the efficient management of each Division.

HEARINGS & SITTINGS via the ADJUDICATIONS DIVISION
12. The format and conduct of any meetings, sittings or hearings undertaken by the Adjudicating Division may be decided by the A.D. Councillors as appropriate to the type of meeting, sitting or hearing being conducted.

13. For the purposes of openness and transparency no PTI hearing or sitting will be held 'in secret', 'in private' or '*in camera*' other than in the case of mediation or arbitration services where both parties have freely requested confidentiality.

14. In the case of such confidentiality being requested, and with the agreement of the PTI Arbitrator or Mediator, no PTI record of the conversations in any such confidential meetings will be made.

15. With the exception of Article 13 above, all hearings or sittings of a fact-finding or judicial nature shall be held in public in venues that are public, and any-and-all parties to any such sittings will be made aware of the same as a precondition of participation. All such hearings will be recorded in digital format as far as facilities allow.

16. Records of all PTI public hearings and sittings, and of Council meetings, will be made available to the public.

APPEALS

17. Given the clarity of PTI submissions guidelines and the fact that PTI final Rulings will *only* be constructed strictly according to existing positive law; there is limited rationale for any appeal mechanism that would almost certainly arrive at the same conclusion. However, this does not preclude the possibility of error or the discovery of relevant laws that were overlooked in the PTI process, which could have had a bearing on the case. Accordingly, a formal, albeit limited appeal process should be in place.

18. Given the narrow scope of any such appeal, and in the interests of practicality, only *final* decisions or Rulings of the Council (vs interim decisions) are open to appeal, and any such appeal will be treated as a case resubmission to be considered at the next QM.

19. Grounds of any such appeal may only refer to; (i) positive law, or (ii) PTI Rules pointing out clearly where an internal action or final Ruling may have been in error.

20. The appeal grounds should be delivered in writing to be read out at Council. The ruling of the Council will be prepared in advance and will be read out in public unless it is deemed necessary and appropriate by the Executive to hold public discussion on the matter beforehand; in which latter case, the agenda, supervision and oversight of any such meeting may be amended accordingly.

21. Should Council (or whichever assigned substitute adjudicating body) find in favour of the appellant, then that finding will be published and the record amended.

22. Should the finding be in favour of the original act or decision (or any other variation other than endorsing the appeal in full) then the Appellant (if not present for the reading) will be notified in writing of the finding and the reasoning thereof, and the same will be made public.

STANDARD DOCUMENTATION *(internal forms in italics)*

In line with the PTI ethos and Mission Statement to endeavour to be an effective and efficient vehicle of remedy as per 'The Overriding Objective', all forms and documentation used by the PTI will be as simple and practical as possible, in standard A4 size for ease of copy.

Wherever possible for example, submissions will be reduced to single, actionable events or incidents so as to facilitate their prompt progression through Council, and all evidence or complimentary documentation will be copied by the submitter to their MCH webpage.

Adjudications Division findings and rulings will likewise be concise, precise and succinct, and will confine themselves purely to written, positive law. It is expected therefore, that even with the addition of the necessary legal caveats and endorsements, that most A.D. rulings, judgments or findings will run to no more than four A4 pages – and preferably, will consist of just 2 or 3 pages.

Form No. **Description**

1	PTI Membership – 1 page
2	General Submission – 1 page plus attachments
3	Case Submission – 3 template pages
4	*Submission Cover Form – 1 page**
5	*Quarterly Submissions List**
6	PTI Council or Divisional Advisory/Notice – 1 page
7	Motion to Council Form – 1 page
8	Adjudicating Division Rulings – 2 to 4 pages

* Internal documents

SECTION SIX

RULES (& GUIDELINES)

The Peoples Tribunal has been set up by dedicated volunteers for specific reasons as outlined in the most recent version of the PTI Mission Statement. Time and resources are limited, so we must operate efficiently, cost-effectively and with full respect to PTI procedures.

It is anticipated that the PTI will come under sustained 'negative attention' from those involved in official misconduct in particular, so as to discredit and undermine the PTI's main objectives.

Some of the methods we are already familiar with are; (a) attempts to disparage, ridicule and belittle using a compliant national press and State-funded broadcasters. (b) Planting disruptors and timewasters within the PTI administration and/or posing fraudulently as prospective complainants and case submitters. (c) Denigrating the PTI's work and findings through the use of internet trolls, false online accounts and propaganda. (d) 'Targeting' key PTI personnel or other PTI Members for various forms of harassment or persecution through the misuse of State resources – most notably via the Garda Siochána, the DPP's Office and the Courts. Accordingly, there are some firm rules that we must all respect – without exception.

1. No changes, alterations, amendments or additions will be made to these Rules that conflict with Section One of this handbook (Ethos) or with the PTI Mission Statement.

2. No matters will come before the PTI Council for formal discussion or consideration at QM's, SCM's or AGM's

except through the Investigations Division or the DCO.

3. The PTI Submissions Form is the ONLY format that will be accepted for Case Submissions (CS).

4. The upfront fee for Case Submissions is compulsory and non-refundable. *(See Section 4, Articles 21 & 41)*

5. All official PTI Correspondence must be on PTI letterhead, duly signed and authorised by the Executive. No formal correspondence will issue out of the PTI in the name of the PTI without prior approval of the Council.

6. Informal correspondence between PTI Admin and original submitting parties in the course of follow-up investigations, research or file compilation (for example) must, in every instance, be signed off by an identifiable PTI Admin, quoting the relevant Case Reference Number.

7. The PTI Logo and title combined, "The Peoples Tribunal of Ireland" (with or without apostrophes) is exclusive to the PTI and may only be reproduced online as; (i) a link to *www.peoplestribunalireland.com*; (ii) accompanying an article that makes reference to the PTI; and/or (iii) as an advertisement to promote the work and activities of the PTI.

8. PTI Members and supporters are asked NOT to criticise other PTI Members or any other anti-corruption activists in public. Disunity plays into the hands of the opposition, so there can be no place in the PTI membership for *public* dissent or criticisms of other activists or groups.

9. The public PTI website is open to all, and anyone can sign up to our email and webtext database.

10. PTI Panel membership is open to anyone who supplies us with their name, address, phone number, email and copy of verifiable photo I.D.

11. Anyone who submits a valid Case Submission Form complete with photo I.D. and submission fee automatically qualifies for the PTI Panel and for their own private webpage at *mycasehistory.com*.

12. PTI Membership is unique to each individual, and is not to be transferred or shared.

13. Membership is voluntary and may be resigned or abandoned at any time, for any reason, by the Member.

14. Membership may not be suspended, revoked, cancelled or rescinded by the PTI Council other than on valid grounds to do with explicit violations of these Rules.

15. The PTI is a lawful entity whose official actions and activities must be sanctioned by Council. Therefore, the PTI and/or any directly-affiliated agency, association or individual is not responsible for the independent actions of any other individual member, or group of members.

16. With the exception of the Executive acting under these Rules, no PTI Member or group of Members may claim to represent PTI or speak on its behalf, but members (as stand-alone persons) are encouraged to declare their membership; to quote directly from the PTI website; and to promote the PTI's work and activities.

17. Case Submissions where any Member of PTI Admin is (i) a named party, or (ii) has any direct, personal interest must be approved in advance, on Motion to the Council.

18. Provision will be made on the PTI website for the publication of *qualified opinions* by any person(s) invited to participate in the production of PTI final Rulings.

19. Dissemination of *unpublished* PTI data or internal materials is expressly forbidden.

20. When engaged in any PTI-sponsored event, activity,

meeting or hearing PTI members undertake to behave in a respectful and law-abiding manner.

21. The PTI Council does not sanction illegal or unlawful conduct. Members who engage in such do so under their own cognizance and may have their membership suspended or revoked as a consequence.

22. **Internal Disputes / Discipline etc.** Hopefully, there will be no real need to enforce any disciplinary measures, as long as the PTI Constitution and Guidelines are clear enough. But in the event that any serious arguments or disputes arise that concern the overall functioning, probity or integrity of the PTI, or if any given Panel Member acts in a seriously counter-productive manner, then any and all such matters will be dealt with exclusively by the Executive* – either in private or public sitting – as the case may be (but preferably private for obvious reasons), and their decision will be binding. *Members will sign off on a clause about this in their application form.*

23. Powers of the Executive in any such disciplinary cases will include; (i) direct arbitration or mediation between disputing parties; (ii) offering an advisory finding (oral or written) on the PTI unconstitutionality of the disputed action; and finally, if necessary, (iii) a sanction in the form of suspension of PTI Panel Membership for any period up to and/or including the next AGM.

24. Suspension by the Executive may be challenged in writing by the Member concerned, and/or by any Councillor, whereupon the matter will be put to majority Council vote. If endorsed, the suspension will stand. If not, the Member will have full privileges restored.

25. Any individual whose Membership has been suspended may play no part in PTI operations during the

period of suspension. However, if the term of their suspension overlaps an AGM, the suspended Member may apply for restoration to the next incoming Council, who will then have the opportunity to discuss and vote on the matter at a suitable time and place.

26. In any disciplinary case that attracts expulsion as a consequence, a formal hearing will be heard at the earliest opportunity but certainly not past the next scheduled QM, SCM or AGM and before not less than 7 Members of Council to include at least 2 Members of the Executive whose decision made by majority vote (by secret ballot if required) must be endorsed by the Executive, and respected by the general PTI Membership.

27. No elected member of the Council may be suspended or removed from the PTI Admin other than; (i) in a case of a serious and critical violation of the Rules, and (ii) by a majority vote of the Council at an EGM that is convened by the Executive for the express purposes of considering the tenure of the said Councillor, and (iii) which majority Council decision must also be endorsed by a majority vote of the Operations Officers (i.e. 51% or more of a potential 40 votes) before it can take effect.

28. Public complaints about any PTI process, procedure or in reference to the handling of any submission or pertaining to the conduct of any PTI Admin in the course of the same may be addressed "c/o The PTI Executive". Such matters will be dealt with professionally and with discretion, with appropriate regard for the respective positions of the parties involved, on a case-by-case basis.

29. Suggestions, advice, constructive criticisms, general commentary or testimonials regarding the PTI and its operations may also be addressed "c/o The PTI Executive" who may publicise the same, as appropriate.

J.U.S.T.I.C.E. GUIDELINES

In addition to other practical measures such as conducting all PTI business in clear, common English (vs legalese for example) and producing rulings and findings that align expressly with written, positive law, the PTI asks all members to consider the following guidelines especially in their dealings with each other.

J = JUSTICE vs INJUSTICE: Although we do not 'practice law' the PTI deals with issues of law and with individual incidences of injustice. As such, anybody who has lodged a legitimate submission or application to the Panel can avail of the facilities of the Peoples Tribunal of Ireland.

U = UNITY & SOLIDARITY: Some of the agencies and institutions whose activities we are challenging are headed by some of the most influential and powerful people in Ireland. To a greater-or-lesser extent these people control law enforcement, the justice system and the media either directly or through indirect influence. This is why it can be so terribly frustrating for the individual citizen to make any headway when faced with collusion, corruption and cronyism amongst the protected elite. It is therefore very important that we (as a group or as individuals) do NOT give unscrupulous persons any ammunition by which to attack or discredit us. Our power lies in our unity as a cohesive, determined group of law-abiding persons who are only seeking our legitimate Constitutional rights under the Rule of Law, and we have to behave as such.

S = STEADFASTNESS & DETERMINATION: We are in this for the long haul folks! We have to be, because the injustices we are confronting are deeply embedded in State institutions, and those responsible are not simply going to roll over, apologise and go away just because we are challenging and exposing them. An absolute determination and a faith in our legitimate cause is therefore key to our long-term success, as well as a planned, systematic and unified approach.

T = TRUTH & OBJECTIVITY: There are a range of outlets—including several online blogs—where wronged citizens can vent their anger and frustration, and name and shame the authority figures responsible for their travails. But if any given individual posts or publishes any inaccuracies, exaggerations or unsubstantiated allegations online or elsewhere, this opens the opportunity for counter-accusations of defamation / hate speech / harassment etc – such as those used by ONE solicitor to shut down the whole of the 'www.rate-your-solicitor.com' website through the Irish Courts. As a result, a very informative website containing many valid reports of serious impropriety by various 'legal professionals' was 'lawfully' removed from public access. This is also why the *mycasehistory* online facility being provided to PTI Members is owned and controlled by *you* and not by us. Each member is responsible for the contents, so *only that member* can be held accountable.

I = INTEGRITY & PROFESSIONALISM: The only way the Peoples Tribunal can function effectively on behalf of the people whilst maintaining the respect of objective observers is to be absolutely scrupulous in presenting a fair, reasonable and fact-based platform that is beyond direct criticism by those who would prefer that the truth be suppressed. So, we ask PTI members who wish to attend public functions (such as domestic Court hearings, or PTI public meetings or sittings) to show courtesy and respect for the authority figures, institutions and agencies we are dealing with – at least until such time as they demonstrate *at an individual level* that they are undeserving of such respect. And even then, we must endeavour to maintain our own dignity and gain the respect of objective observers, or else risk being denounced as cranks and complainers, and thereby lose our hard-won popular support.

C = COMPASSION & CONSIDERATION: We also ask that PTI members show respect and support for each other – most especially at public events, at PTI meetings and at domestic Court appearances. Our strength lies in our unified position against corruption and criminality, not in differing opinions about the particular merits of each other's positions, personalities or circumstances. We need to focus on the issues – and in particular, the terrible wrongs that have been done to fellow citizens. There is hardly a member of the PTI (or closely-affiliated groups) who has not suffered considerably at the hands of unscrupulous authority figures. The wounds inflicted by those experiences, be they physical, emotional or psychological, often run very deep, so it is important that we are compassionate, tolerant and supportive of each other, and that we keep our criticisms or any 'unhelpful' or divisive commentary to the minimum.

E = EFFECTIVE TACTICS: The Council members and Operations Officers who guide the activities of the PTI have invested a great deal of time and effort into developing processes and procedures that will be of genuine assistance to citizens who find themselves subject to unjust, illegal or prejudicial activities by compromised authority figures. Please respect those efforts and feel free to offer constructive criticism or suggestions where needed. But the key to success is that we all use these methods in a unified and determined way, trusting in the collective support of the PTI membership and the approval of all decent people.

SECTION SEVEN

THE LEGAL CASE FOR THE ESTABLISHMENT OF THE PEOPLES TRIBUNAL OF IRELAND IN ACCORDANCE WITH THE RULE OF LAW
(and of associated matters)

*   *   *

A FORMAL DECLARATION

Sent 'under seal' to the President of Ireland and the Council of State; to the Members of the 33rd Dáil; 'cc' all senior officials and office holders in the Irish State, July 2020.

The sovereignty and legitimacy of any State is defined by—and is dependent upon—that State's adherence to 'a rule of law' by which the government asserts and maintains its authority. In the case of member States of the United Nations, of the Council of Europe and of the European Union, membership of these bodies is dependent not merely upon the fact (or claim) that there is *a* rule of law or that "rule *by* law" exists in that State, but upon each Member States' declared respect for, and statutory application of "*the* Rule of Law" and the parallel values of democracy, human rights, social justice and economic freedom which combined concepts underpin the collective political morality of those institutions.

Consequently, if it can be shown that a Member State of the UN, the CoE or EU does NOT respect or abide by the Rule of Law – or indeed that there exists a chronic failure to even properly maintain any consistent rule *of* law or rule *by* law – then clearly that State is suffering a crisis of sovereignty and statutory legitimacy sufficient to challenge its continued membership of those institutions, at least until such time as the Rule of Law is properly re-established and is being fully and effectively applied.

The primary purpose of this Declaration is to place 'on the record' in one concise document:

(i)   The legal grounds and conditions upon which *The Peoples' Tribunal of Ireland* has been established.

(ii)   The requirement that the Irish Government establishes without delay a *Part 2 Enquiry* under the terms of *the Houses of the Oireachtas (Inquiries, Privileges and Procedures) Act 2013* as referenced herein, and upon the factual contents and commentary contained in the attached I-I Report, *"CRIMINALITY IN THE IRISH COURTS – And the Absence of the Rule of Law".*

(iii) To provide to the UN General Assembly, the Council of Europe and the EU Commission the materials necessary to take the appropriate action to ensure that the Irish State returns to a position of full and proper compliance with the Rule of Law, and by association, with its sworn obligations under UN, CoE and EU membership, or, to endure the prescribed consequences of failing to do so.

1. THE ABSENCE OF THE RULE OF LAW IN IRELAND

We respectfully draw your attention to the attached 98-page condensed 'I-I Report' (Integrity Ireland Report sent by email) entitled *"Criminality in the Irish Courts – And the Absence of the Rule of Law"*, Part One of which was served on all Irish authorities and on the Petitions Committee of the European Parliament in January 2020. In the absence of any proper responses, the condensed 98-page PDF version was served again in July 2020 on the newly-formed incoming Irish government and the full 270-page Report was officially published [ISBN: 978-1-906628-88-8]. That published 'I-I Report' contains additional proofs and evidence in support of the overall theme; that there is a crisis of endemic and systemic criminality in the institutions of the Irish State and a documented absence of the Rule of Law.

Scope of the Report

Of necessity, that pilot Report deals with a succession of interconnected events experienced by just one individual and his family over a period of several years. Other cases known to the *Integrity Ireland Association* with comparable identifiers – some of which include several of the named accused as well as other repeat offenders – were not included in that launch publication due to the necessity to have just one source of authorship; one locus for confirmations; and just one target for anticipated reprisals by the establishment including disreputable attempts to suppress, deny, or denounce the contents – and/or to discredit and vilify the author – such as in the cases of Sgt Maurice McCabe and others.

Summary

That I-I Report documents the disturbing fact that we have, over a period of several years now, made all manner of lawful approaches – both formal and informal

– to the Irish statutory authorities and to other agencies and oversight bodies; to address numerous documented incidences of unlawful and unconstitutional behaviour including serious, repeat, criminal activities by persons in the employ of the Irish State (and/or in the pay of the State) noting that the persistence and frequency of the said illicit behaviour and the corresponding failures and refusals of the respective authorities to deal with prohibited conduct according to the law has resulted in the alarming circumstances where the requisite 'Rule of Law' is not in effect being respected, applied or adhered to in any recognisably-consistent or equitable manner sufficient to qualify the Irish State as having, *"a properly functioning justice system"* complete with, *"competent, lawfully-established domestic Courts with effective appeal mechanisms"* that are overseen by, *"a politically-independent judiciary who abide by the law"*; such as is required under the Irish Constitution and which said national political status is mandatory for membership of; (a) the European Union, (b) the Council of Europe, and (c) the United Nations.

Methodology & Evidence
For the avoidance of any doubt; our lawful approaches to the statutory authorities over a 10+ year period are detailed in numerous letters, formal complaints and in affidavits on the public record in the Superior Courts, and include (but are not limited to) the following:

- Lodging criminal complaints with An Garda Síochána and Garda HQ (Irish police).

- Lodging formal complaints to internal authorities within each agency or affiliate business, including to: the Law Society; the Bar Council; the CEO of the Courts Service; An Post; HSE/TUSLA; the DPP's Office; to various Ministers of State; to the named

Presidents of the Courts; the respective Taoisigh; and to Michael D Higgins, President of Ireland.

- Seeking support and assistance and initiating follow-up complaints and enquiries with the respective 'Statutory Oversight Bodies' including to the Minister for Justice; the Garda Commissioner; the Ombudsman; the Information Commissioner; the Garda Síochána Ombudsman Commission; the Chief of Staff of the Defence Forces; the Irish Human Rights Commission; the Department of Justice Review Panel; the DPP, and the Charleton Tribunal.

- Contacting ALL of the firms of solicitors listed on the Criminal legal Aid Panel and making direct contact with 1,874 Irish Barristers for the purposes of seeking legal representation.

- Pursuing private civil and criminal actions in the Courts.

- Lodging numerous applications and appeals to the Superior Courts.

- Making formal applications to the European Court of Human Rights.

- Writing to all sitting TD's, Ministers of State and sitting Judges.

- Lodging a petition with the European Parliament.

- Sending, offering, or making available to all of the said parties, physical evidence and other unchallengeable proofs of the criminality alleged.

- Initiating valid citizens' arrests of a number of officials and office holders.

- Making dozens of valid applications for criminal summonses under *S.10 of the Petty Sessions Act,* and, when unlawfully refused, rejected or ignored, and/or when refused entry to the Courts by gardaí; by following up via alternative lawful processes such as here listed.

- Setting up the *Integrity Ireland Association* in support of victims and survivors of State-sponsored illegalities, and to lobby the Irish authorities for civil justice and political reform.

- Placing a series of formal 'QTC' Notices & Declarations on the record for the purposes of legal clarity, transparency and accountability. *(See I-I Report pp.220-225).*

- Collaborating with 'like-minded others' including concerned citizens and residents of the State who have had proven, damaging experience of the Irish Courts and who seek urgent reform of the institutions of State so as to align truthfully and credibly with the Rule of Law.

Almost without exception, each of these lawful efforts have met with coordinated unlawful resistance and obstructionism by the Irish establishment – and in particular (in the cases outlined in the I-I Report) by the named accused parties—sometimes serially so—which in turn has provided incontestable evidence of repeat, systemic attempts to interfere with, obstruct, pervert and/or deny justice for the primary purposes of; (i) visiting unlawful and unwanted attentions on otherwise innocent parties, and/or (ii) shielding from exposure or accountability, persons in the employ of the State (or affiliates thereof) who are undeniably guilty of criminal acts.

We further note, explicitly, that in attempting to avail of our fundamental right to access justice, that we have now 'exhausted all domestic remedies' in seeking the rights due to us under the Rule of Law, and that the Irish State – chiefly in the form of the Department of Justice in context of its supervisory and oversight functions over the various arms of the Department – has completely and utterly failed in its constitutional duties to uphold the Rule of Law and protect our fundamental rights. Indeed, that three Ministers of Justice in succession have either failed or refused to act on documented proofs of serious criminality by their agents and affiliates and/or have engaged in further criminal activity for the purposes of unlawfully suppressing and covering-up multiple proven, documented crimes – particularly regarding the obstruction of justice; the perversion of justice; and/or by interfering with the due and lawful administration of justice – which said offences have been committed variously by their colleagues, subordinates, and professional associates.

In context, we refer to the legislation quoted at Chapters 1 – 5 of the I-I Report which not only requires residents and citizens of this State: (a) NOT to engage knowingly and directly in criminal activity; (b) NOT to facilitate or cover-up criminal activity; and (c) NOT to deliberately impede criminal investigations or prosecutions in the Courts; but (d) to actively report the same when knowledge of specific criminality comes to their attention. For example:

Criminal Justice Act 2011: S.19. [withholding information]—(1) A person shall be guilty of an offence if he or she has information which he or she knows or believes might be of material assistance in—(a) preventing the commission by any other person of a relevant offence, or (b) securing the apprehension, prosecution or conviction of any other person for a relevant offence, and fails without reasonable excuse to disclose that information as soon as it is practicable to do so to a member of the Garda Síochána.

S.17. [concealing facts disclosed by documents]—(1) Any person who—(a) knows or suspects that an investigation by the Garda Síochána into a relevant offence, other than an offence to which section 51 of the Criminal Justice (Theft and Fraud Offences) Act 2001 applies, is being or is likely to be carried out, and (b) falsifies, conceals, destroys or otherwise disposes of a document or record which he or she knows or suspects is or would be relevant to the investigation or causes or permits its falsification, concealment, destruction or disposal, shall be guilty of an offence.

(2) Where a person—(a) falsifies, conceals, destroys or otherwise disposes of a document, or (b) causes or permits its falsification, concealment, destruction or disposal, in such circumstances that it is reasonable to conclude that the person knew or suspected—(i) that an investigation by the Garda Síochána into a relevant offence.. ...applies, was being or was likely to be carried out, and (ii) that the document was or would be relevant to the investigation, he or she shall be taken for the purposes of this section to have so known or suspected, unless the court or the jury, as the case may be, is satisfied having regard to all the evidence that there is a reasonable doubt as to whether he or she so knew or suspected.

Criminal Damage Act 1991: S.2. (3) A person who damages any property, whether belonging to himself or another, with intent to defraud shall be guilty of an offence.

The fact that these, and many such similar offences as listed in the I-I Report have been reported via official channels without any consequent sanctions or prosecutions of the named accused should be sufficient to raise alarm bells in the minds of any decent, right-thinking, law-abiding persons, and especially amongst those persons whose duty is to uphold the Rule of Law in this State. We note in particular that a number of valid applications for criminal summonses under *S.10 of the Petty Sessions Act 1851* remain inexplicably (and unlawfully) 'on hold' in the Criminal Courts of Justice which said applications name several senior officials and office holders in proven criminal activity. That these are among many such valid applications which have met with coordinated, unlawful obstructionism by the very persons empowered and mandated to 'uphold the law and the constitution' and that despite these illicit activities being in overt, flagrant breach of Superior Court rulings and judgments as recent as 2016 (as listed at p.20 of this Declaration) that even the Superior Courts are now actively complicit in the suppression of these criminal applications and of the incontestable facts that ground them; leading to additional published accusations and charges as against those persons involved in unlawful, underhanded and disreputable 'business' in the Courts.

> **Criminal Law Act 1997**: *S.7.(2) Where a person has committed an arrestable offence, any other person who, knowing or believing him or her to be guilty of the offence or of some other arrestable offence, does without reasonable excuse any act with intent to impede his or her apprehension or prosecution shall be guilty of an offence.*

Similar legislation is unequivocal as to what constitutes an offence under the law, including any additional acts of criminal concealment, obstructionism or denial of the facts which often includes collusive attempts to pervert justice via acts of perjury, fraud, conspiracy to deceive, to abuse due process and other unsanctioned contempts of Court, as well as serial obfuscations on the part of various 'Officers of the Court' for the purposes of exhausting the resources and resolve of otherwise credible complainants and litigants, which said offences are covered for example in *The Criminal Justice (Theft & Fraud Offences) Act, 2001* which, at S.6 explicitly states:

> *"(1) A person who dishonestly, with the intention of making a gain for himself or herself or another, or of causing loss to another, by any deception induces another to do or refrain from doing an act, is guilty of an offence."*

Conclusion: On the basis of the evidence supplied and in the interests of expediency and clarity; it can accurately be summarised that the current, actual circumstances in Ireland are that a sizeable majority of senior officials and office holders – particularly in the justice-related arena – are actively involved in; (a) the commission of criminal acts; and/or (b) the concealment and cover-ups of those acts; and/or (c) in the unlawful 'targeting' by way of criminal harassment and focused persecution of persons who are perceived to be a threat to the unchallenged continuation of the said criminal activities.

In short, that the evidence in the said I-I Report establishes beyond any reasonable doubt the existence of a *de facto* 'criminal organisation' (as per the respective statutory descriptions) operating undeclared within the auspices of the Irish justice system, wherein the individuals so involved are masquerading as 'officials and office holders' while illegitimately drawing down the benefits and supports due to those offices whilst simultaneously abusing the powers and authority available to them and violating the terms and responsibilities of those offices in knowing contravention of the Rule of Law, for the purposes of advancing collaborative, definitive, predetermined criminal ends.

This leads us inexorably to the unsavoury question as to how many persons need to be involved in this criminal activity – and for how long and at what cost to the public, before we call a spade, a damned spade?

> **"'Criminal organisation' means a structured group, however organised, composed of 3 or more persons acting in concert, that has as its main purpose or activity the commission or facilitation of one or more serious offences in order to obtain, directly or indirectly, a financial or other material benefit. 'Act' includes omission; and a reference to the commission or doing of an act includes a reference to the making of an omission."**
>
> *Abridged, from: The Criminal Justice Act 2006 & 2009 & the UN Convention against Transnational Organized Crime 2000.*

Given the evidence provided, there can be no credible rebuttal to the claim that the Rule of Law is not – and has not – been applied in the conduct of these sample cases in this pilot Report, and, inasmuch as senior office holders with the statutory responsibility to address these critical failings have not only failed and refused to do so, but have repeatedly abused their positions to compound the crimes already committed, and have thereby rendered themselves subject to accusation and indictment; that the parallel allegation that a veritable 'criminal organisation' comprising so-called 'Officers of the Court' and their associates in the legal profession which subsists and indeed even thrives in the midst of our justice system under political patronage and statutory protection begs the inescapable question as to how much of this malfeasance needs to be occurring, for what amount of time and at what depth and persistence, and at how high the positions before we unequivocally declare and accept the glaring reality; that other than in theory and being simply 'written on paper' that there is in effect no actual, genuine Rule of Law in Ireland?

This is an inescapable reality bound by serious questions that simply cannot be ignored if we are to maintain any national dignity or credibility on the world stage. This point having been clearly made; let us now review other aspects of the problem with a view to identifying credible and achievable solutions.

2. THE INHERENT LEGITIMACY OF OFFICES & INSTITUTIONS OF STATE

First of all we note the indisputable, self-evident fact that the tenure of any-and-all officials and office holders in this State is contingent upon their individual adherence to the Rule of Law and their respective positions as citizens of this State who are each, "subject to the law and the Constitution". Indeed, that the very existence of this State and its legal standing as a sovereign nation, as well as its continued membership of the European Union is predicated upon its adherence to the Rule of Law.

We further note that the various 'Offices of State' in-and-of-themselves are meaningless entities without an assigned, named 'Office Holder' who has the overall responsibility to direct, administer and supervise that Office's activities according to the law and the Constitution. Accordingly, any such prevailing 'responsibilities of office' rest entirely on the incumbent office holder and the validity and authority of any such Office is entirely dependent upon the respective office holder's capacity, willingness and ability to carry out the functions of their Office according to the Rule of Law.

Conversely, should any assigned office holder prove incapable, unable or unwilling to carry out the functions of their Office, then naturally—as is provided for in *Article 35.4(i) of the Constitution* in the case of judges for example—those persons may be removed from Office on the grounds of 'incapacity'. And whilst it must be understood of course, that all such office holders are human, fallible and imperfect beings who may from time to time suffer lapses, errors or other failings of office that can reasonably be excepted to occur and therefore should, in most cases, be accepted and overlooked as the inevitable consequences of employing people rather than robots; that any such occasional 'errors or lapses' are vastly different in essence and in consequence, to the more sombre declaration that one is either 'unable or incapable' of carrying out one's statutory functions.

Similarly, any such office holder who engages in 'misconduct' or other inappropriate activities sufficient to jeopardise the authority of their Office, such as knowingly committing criminal offences in context of the same; renders their tenure of that Office immediately invalid, whereupon the said Office is consequently and ineluctably vacated until such time as the invalid office holder is replaced.

It needs to be said of course, that if the said misconduct goes unnoticed or unreported, that the said office holder may physically continue in position unperturbed, albeit as the now-illegitimate holder of an Office whose standing has been compromised and/or corrupted by the office holder's criminal activity. It also needs to be said – somewhat obviously – that if the said misconduct *is* in fact reported to the statutory authorities then there needs to be consequences according to law, otherwise there is in effect, no law at all. And this is the predicament and conundrum that faces those of us who have chosen to live in a modern democratic State, an advanced 'first world' nation and a Member State of the UN, the CoE and the EU, where the Rule of Law is supposed to reign paramount.

3. THE PROBITY, INTEGRITY AND LAWFUL FUNCTIONING OF DOMESTIC COURTS

With no intention of causing gratuitous offence or indeed of indulging in any exaggeration or overstatement, it needs to be said, quite objectively and dispassionately, that the circumstances we find ourselves in (as detailed in the I-I Report) are so far removed from any notion of 'the Rule of Law' or of genuine 'access to justice' – as to render the prospect of approaching the Irish Courts for a lawful remedy in any matters that threaten to expose the rampant misconduct, corruption and criminality ongoing 'in high places' to be utterly futile and pointless. The machinery of the law it seems, is not actually there to serve justice; but the interests of connected elites. If one finds oneself by misfortune (or otherwise) in opposition to this cabal – well, prayer may well be one's only option.

With due regard and respect to those individuals judges who may indeed aspire to ethical conduct, those of us with intimate experience of the Superior Courts have come to the inescapable conclusion that there is so much dishonesty, deliberate rule-breaking and blatant criminal contempt for the law going on in those elevated chambers as to render the Irish Courts in general 'unfit for purpose' and to render specific Courts legally redundant, and particular named judges to be morally defunct and therefore plainly, 'unfit for office'.

The European Court of Justice (ECJ) established 6 criteria for the recognition of 'a competent domestic tribunal' to include the national Courts of Member States. *(Case C54/96 & C-196/09)* These ask the following questions concerning the said Court(s):

1. Is it established by law?
2. Is it permanent?
3. Is its jurisdiction compulsory?
4. Does it have an inter-partes procedure?
5. Does it apply rules of law?
6. Is it independent?

ASSESMENT OF IRISH COURTS AGAINST THESE CRITERIA
Point No 1 requires that the Court, "is established by law". Unfortunately, no-one can produce the original *Commencement Order No 1* for the *1924 Courts of Justice Act,* which is *the* mother document that granted 'jurisdiction' (the lawful right and authority to operate) on all Irish Courts. This means, technically-and-literally, that there is NO evidence that our Courts were ever given legal standing by the Government of the day. Notwithstanding the mindboggling scenario that this 'fact' presents us with, and the consequent bearing it has on *all* of the court cases heard between 1924 and 1961, and, since then, *all* of the cases that were initiated in the lower Courts; the plain fact of the matter is that if *Commencement Order No 1 of 1924* was never actually enacted (which does seem to be the case) then certainly, our Courts are not what they appear to be no matter what the optics are. Yes, we have buildings that look like Courts, and we have lots of pretentious-looking people in wigs and gowns getting well-paid by the public to swan around with highfalutin airs and graces – and some of them even make legal pronouncements that are

enforced by gardaí and bailiffs, but unfortunately, it may all be utterly invalid and void – all the way back to 1924! Common sense would suggest that we should put the question to the people as to what should be done, but instead, the legal establishment has now decreed that the *1961 Courts (Supplemental Provisions) Act*, (which was actually grounded on the non-existent 1924 Act with nearly 40 direct references to it) has somehow since remedied the absence of any vested jurisdiction by simply carrying-over and amending legislation that was never even enacted in the first place!? Only the lawyers could have come up with that one! To be clear, the establishment is now trying to dismiss the inconvenient historical illegality of our Courts by simply ignoring the fact that the 1924 Act was never commenced, thereby putting an even bigger spotlight on an issue that raises questions about the overall legitimacy and legal standing of all Irish Courts today.

Raising this particular issue here may seem to be pettifogging in circumstances where we are arguing about the far more important principle of the very existence of the Rule of Law in Ireland – especially when our other points of contention are far more contemporarily (vs historically) relevant – but in circumstances where we are challenging the overall legitimacy of the Irish Courts as they stand and operate today, this technical-legal point simply had to be addressed and included. For a better understanding as to how the law relates to 'Void' or non-existent Court Orders or other legal nullities, please see *"V: The Void Court Order"* on page 23 of the I-I Report.

Point No 2 requires that the Court, "is permanent". But arguably (apart from those wonderful gothic buildings left to us by the British and the glitzy C.C.J. in Dublin) our

Courts as legal institutions may not be 'permanent' *per-se* inasmuch as they appear NOT to have been granted jurisdiction in 1924 and thereby would have had NO domestic, statutory, legal validity to operate.

Point No 3 requires that the Court, "has compulsory jurisdiction". Unfortunately, like many legal terms, this one is somewhat indistinct and open to interpretation. 'Compulsory' for example can mean, "an essential component required to operate" or, it can imply that some sort of force (such as the threat of arrest, or fines, or seizure of property) may be deployed in order to compel compliance – right? 'Jurisdiction' is defined as, "the extent of the power to make legal decisions and judgments". So, the phrase, "the Court has compulsory jurisdiction" could be understood as saying that; (i) jurisdiction *must be* bestowed upon the Court by the Government, and without it the Court *cannot* operate (which is a lawful fact); and/or (ii) that, under pain of penalty, the public is obliged to obey the rulings of the Court according to the limits of that Court's 'jurisdiction' (which is another lawful fact). 'Jurisdiction' in this latter context includes the Court's geographical location, the types of cases it can deal with, and/or the size of any penalty or damages award etc). But the immediate pressing question is, how can something that may not be lawfully in existence in the first place, have any sort of 'compulsory jurisdiction'? In addition, and setting aside the 1924 Act issue for a moment, adherence to the judicial oath of office is an absolute requirement for a judge's *vested* (personal) jurisdiction under *Article 34*. Accordingly, if as has been shown, our Courts are largely preoccupied with the covering up or facilitation of official crime, and in so doing, that various 'Officers of the Court' including named judges are indulging in deliberate criminal activity..? Well obviously, this renders any purported 'jurisdiction' of that particular judge *and* of that Court—let alone any so-called "*compulsory* jurisdiction"—immediately invalid; that is, other than in the minds of a largely-ignorant, confused and deceived public who live in fear of the consequences (police, fines, jail, losing loved ones into State care, etc..) of challenging this illegitimate cabal – or when refusing to comply with its unlawful diktats?

Point No 4 requires that the Court, "has an inter-partes procedure". This point is conceded inasmuch as our Courts are primarily structured to deal with cases on an adversarial basis between prosecuting and defending parties – which arguably, is not the most conducive environment to expedite justice. Many would argue for a more collaborative approach (especially in non-criminal cases) where joint resolutions could be agreed. On the other hand however, a confrontational setting does tend to increase costs and fees. In any event, this 'inter-partes' (Latin) requirement is supposed to be there to ensure that no one can win or lose a case without 'due process' and without a chance to have their say. What is not elucidated here is the fact that most legally-untrained persons who enter an Irish Court are immediately at an inter-partes disadvantage precisely *because* of the deliberately obscure and obtuse language being used, because of the confrontational setting, and because they are utterly bewildered by the tortuous, convoluted pantomime unfolding around them. Whatever 'inter-partes' procedure they may actually 'participate in' is solely through their legal representative who may (and more often, may not) value a client's interests over his commission from the case. Other factors may gravely affect any supposed 'effective legal representation' of an all-but-dumb client. In short, it is our experience that simply having an 'inter-partes' procedure in place is no guarantee of genuine representation, nor of a fair hearing in an Irish Court, especially when so many other routine violations of truth, law and justice are being systematically ignored or disingenuously facilitated.

Point No 5 requires that the Court, "applies rules of law". Unfortunately, and based on our collective experience to date and upon all of the evidence in the I-I Report, it is clear that Irish judges do not apply 'rules of law' in any recognisably consistent or reliable basis. Some judges may, but most do not, simply because they don't have to. This is partly because of the stranglehold that 'The Benchers' hold over the legal profession and the career consequences for individual lawyers if-and-when they ever muster the courage to challenge judicial errors there-and-then in the Courtroom, especially when the more profitable alternative (for everyone but the bewildered litigant) is to rack up endless appeal fees in the Superior Courts. Furthermore, when law is actually being applied (as opposed to when it is being completely and utterly ignored) it is usually being applied 'prejudicially and selectively' in favour of whichever party to the case has the requisite political influence or statutory locus, which blatant, thinly-veiled bias makes a complete nonsense of the concept and principle of, "applying the law – without fear or favour".

Point No 6 requires the Court to be, "independent". The inconvenient fact that Irish Judges are politically appointed in a most brazen fashion makes a complete nonsense of this requirement. Despite paltry efforts by the establishment to conceal these sleights-of-hand through supposed 'robust independent recruitment and selection procedures' such as the admittedly "pointless and redundant" Judicial Advisory Appointments Board

(JAAB) which hasn't even held *one* formal interview in some 25 years of its existence, is statement enough. The added fact that even the tame national press opined; *"The JAAB camouflage is a laughable layer of obfuscation"* with its Board top-heavy with Judges, is sufficient to make the point that the JAAB is mere political tokenism wrapped up in smoke-and-mirrors designed to deceive and mislead the public. The plain, undeniable fact is that Irish judges are politically appointed, and remain embedded in the establishment. Accordingly, there is no genuine separation of powers. Period. *(See I-I Report p.72)*

To conclude this Section: It is our sincere position that the Irish Courts – as they currently stand – do not adequately fulfil these EU/ECJ criteria thus leaving Ireland without 'a competent domestic tribunal' or indeed without any properly-functioning justice system, which, if proven, would further endorse the requirement for an immediate *Part 2 Enquiry* and qualify the urgent establishment of the Peoples' Tribunal of Ireland.

If we are to accept then, that the EU criteria for 'competent domestic tribunals' are not nearly being met, and that other troubling factors such as outlined here and in the I-I Report raise fundamental questions as to the overall statutory legitimacy of our Courts and of their general operational probity – then surely, someone in authority should be asking the all-too-obvious question as to how did we find ourselves in this sad and sorry mess in the first place, and what are we going to do about it?

Because, if these are not 'lawful courts' by express definition, then they are 'unlawful courts' (at best) and only 'courts' at all by mere virtue of the existence of the court buildings, infrastructure and staff. But these are courts without legal, moral or technical validity because they operate in direct violation of their constitutional terms of operation. For any such unlawful courts to continue to draw upon the resources of the State so as to force compliance with unlawful orders, judgments, instructions or directions under threat of penal consequences for the parties concerned, is of course yet another blatant violation of the constitutional requirement that our Courts (and judges by inseparable association) operate, *"subject to the law and the Constitution"* and, under the Rule of Law.

In conclusion, if we are to assess the overall merits, the probity, the integrity and the legitimacy of the Irish Courts against the 6-point checklist of the European Union, not to mention as against our own internal Court Rules and the *Article 34* requirement that the Courts be 'established according to law' then clearly, we are in a bit of a quagmire at best, and arguably in a serious legal and constitutional crisis that needs to be addressed as a matter of great urgency by the Irish State – and this even, before we take a closer look at the legalities that are contiguous to the Irish judiciary.

4. THE IRISH JUDICIARY: SELECTION, JURISDICTION, INCAPACITY & MISCONDUCT

The I-I Report establishes that a culture of selective contempt for – and abuse of – the law exists in the nation's Courts whereby certain judges in particular feel at liberty to engage in serious judicial misconduct for the purposes of protecting from accountability other agents of the State and/or of otherwise 'connected insiders' who are engaged in improper, corrupt or unlawful activities. Licence also appears to have been given to certain judges and various other 'Officers of the Court' to disrespect, mislead and deceive lay litigants in particular, and generally disregard their fundamental right to, *"a fair and impartial hearing before a competent, independent and impartial tribunal established by law"*. It hardly bears articulation what the fate is of those who are perceived to be 'politically inconvenient' or in any way a threat to the establishment. The role of the judge as a fair and impartial referee in a very lopsided game where the rules and the goalposts are being constantly (and illicitly) changed is practically unheard of, and anyone who is embedded within the State seems impervious to sanction or correction, no matter how grievous their offences against 'the Court' are.

These antagonistic intentions and dishonourable attitudes and behaviours fly directly in the face of the internationally-recognised and UN-endorsed *Bangalore Principles of Judicial Conduct* which should be at the forefront of any statutory considerations in the selection and appointment of persons to the Bench. Unfortunately, and somewhat ridiculously here in Ireland (and other than the general *pretence* of propriety which certain Irish judges are so adept at) it is the notable *absence* of those core values of, "independence, impartiality, integrity, propriety, equality, competence and diligence" that seems the best guarantee of being selected by one's political patrons or colleagues in the legal profession for a cosy appointment to the Bench. The fact that certain judges have appalling records in their previous careers as solicitors or barristers is telling enough. The added fact that they do NOT have to disclose their personal 'interests' (financial or otherwise) leaves open the suspicion and possibility (which has been proven a number of times) that any given judge could be subject to influence, pressure or profit such as to interfere with their supposed 'statutory independence'. But it is the accumulation of scores of serious complaints by ordinary members of the public that marks the overwhelming majority of Irish judges as having been politically appointed in the first place, with the clear, yet undeclared expectation – as is generally proven in their subsequent actions – that the protection of the status quo, however corrupt, trumps any naïve notions they might have of justice, impartiality or integrity. And whilst we must always make allowances for the exception to the rule, it is abundantly clear that 'the rule' here in Ireland is that if you are NOT politically connected, and you are NOT willing to bat for the status quo, then you probably aren't going to find yourself on any Bencher's shortlist anytime soon. That is an appalling indictment of a profession that is supposed to comprise the very best of us; those who are genuinely wise, independent, impartial and fair; the guardians of law; and persons whose honesty and integrity can always and absolutely be relied upon.

Notwithstanding the unsettling backdrop of political insiderism in the judicial appointments process, statutory factors endow Irish Courts with the legal authority and jurisdiction to administer justice. These are laid out in the Constitution under Articles 34–38 and include (abridged):

- That Courts are set up according to law and operate within their respective jurisdictions. *[Article 34.1.]*
- That individual judges obey the law, respect the Constitution, and act within jurisdiction. *[Article 34.5(i)]*
- That judges abide strictly by their solemn Constitutional Oath of Office. *[Article 34.5(i)]*
- That judges respect the order of primacy of law, and comply with Superior Courts' Rulings.

- That judges are constitutionally 'capable' of carrying out their duties. *[Article 35.4(i)]*

- That judges do NOT engage in 'misbehaviour'. *[Article 35.4(i)]*

The constitutional requirement that judges are 'capable' of carrying out their duties requires an understanding of the physical, logistical, educational, and psychological demands of the role of judge. Accordingly, anyone who is technically 'incapable' of carrying out that role should not be appointed, or, if they demonstrate by their behaviour that they are incapable, then according to the constitution, they may / shall / should be removed from office. Unfortunately, that is not happening.

Two pertinent issues immediately arise in our collective experience of the Irish Courts. Firstly, we need to acknowledge that a high proportion of those being appointed to the Bench are politically selected, and secondly, that a number of these appointees suffer from what is currently known as, 'antisocial personality disorder' or ASPD. This is a condition recognised by the *Diagnostic and Statistical Manual of Mental Disorders (DSM-5)* and is more commonly referred to as 'sociopathy' or 'psychopathy'. It is our position that persons so afflicted are entirely unsuitable for judicial office on the grounds that; (a) such a diagnosis renders them literally-and-psychologically 'incapable' of performing certain functions; and (b) that persons so afflicted are predicated towards certain typical behaviours – many of which result in actions that fall well beyond the bounds of mere 'misconduct'.

To clarify: In context of the lawful functioning of our Courts, it needs to be pointed out that the judges' oath of office (which is an absolute prerequisite for vested jurisdiction) has three identifiable aspects: (a) the literal-legal aspect that requires some academic awareness of how to correctly, "uphold the law – without fear or favour"; (b) an ethical-moral aspect that guides that proper application; and (c) a religious aspect that renders the oath-taker answerable to God.

Naturally, if the oath-taker is an atheist, then the oath is meaningless. Likewise, if the oath-taker intends to service his political patrons, friends and colleagues through his office at the expense of justice, then again, the oath is meaningless. Finally, if the oath-taker can be shown to be a clinical sociopath or psychopath, then that person is, literally-and-clinically "incapable" (in the constitutional, literal and personal-psychological sense) of accommodating any sworn oath that requires a *genuine* application of ethics, morality, or truth or justice – over one's own self-interests.

In short, whilst it may be understandable that the highest percentage of sociopaths and psychopaths in any given profession (second only to the CEO's of multinational corporations) are in the legal profession, and that any amount of solicitors or lawyers could therefore very well suffer from a disorder that makes lying, deception, theft, fraud, malicious perjuries, and the routine manipulation and exploitation of others just 'normal' behaviour for them; then equally, it needs to be said that the role of judge—as THE very person who must limit and curtail these sociopathic leanings in the Courts in the overall interests of justice—that *that* central role cannot possibly be assigned to yet another nefarious sociopath who may, or may not, actually perceive that any 'wrong' *per se* is being done by their counterparts even in the face of overt lawbreaking – which in any event the judge *should* be acting upon – and *should* be penalising.

The fact that our judges rarely sanction even serious transgressions by other agents of the State is one clear giveaway. But a more disturbing aspect of ASPD is the relative absence of conscience, morals or empathy which is often coupled with sadistic and/or predatory traits and behaviours, all of which when combined in any specific diagnosis of ASPD would most assuredly render the subject not only utterly unfit for high public office, but indeed for any position or role of 'service to the public' that requires honest, empathetic and insightful decision-making, and/or a willingness to protect others from the predatory and often-criminal attentions of one's colleagues in the legal profession.

And this, upon the logical, clinical and obvious premise that empathy is largely absent in the clinical sociopath, and that genuine 'service to others' is simply not in their nature. The *appearance* of service or empathetic concern may be there, but there are no such intentions.

As to stated 'misbehaviour' being grounds for removal from judicial office, obvious examples would include for example; (i) the requirement that judges do NOT abuse their statutory powers or vested jurisdiction (where applicable). (ii) That they do NOT scandalise the Courts or bring the judiciary into disrepute by engaging in unethical, unprincipled, dishonest or disreputable behaviour whilst carrying out their judicial duties; and (iii) that they do NOT act in contempt of their own Courts by knowingly engaging in, or facilitating frauds, deceptions, perjuries and other offences against justice.

Again, with respect to those judges not of our experience who may operate otherwise; it is the very existence and persistence of this sort of criminal misbehaviour by persons who are supposed to be beyond reproach that gives rise to an urgent need for some lawful alternative to these morally-compromised individuals and corrupted institutions which, in the blatant continuance of these illicit and unlawful activities, serves only to mock and abuse the public's faith and confidence in what has since devolved into a nefarious, autocratic farce; a charade dressed up to look like a justice system; a cabal of politically-connected insiders and subservient lackeys who have hijacked the institutions and organs of State for intrinsically dishonest, devious, selfish, malicious and/or criminal purposes.

Hence the truism that if a high proportion of senior judges are knowingly engaging in overt misconduct, misfeasance, malfeasance, deception, nonfeasance and other forms of dishonest and discreditable behaviour sufficient to ground valid allegations of *criminal* misbehaviour, then clearly, it cannot be said that those particular Courts and those particular judges are operating, "subject to the law and the Constitution", which is arguably, *the* preeminent constitutional qualifier of what does, and does not constitute 'a lawful Court' *[Article 34.1.]*. And this, in addition to the questions already raised about the historical legitimacy of the Irish Courts and their alignment with EU criteria.

Furthermore, inasmuch as any such criminal misbehaviour by sitting judges has been observed, documented and reported but nevertheless draws NO statutory responses or remedies from the executive, legislative or judicial branches of the State, then this, somewhat obviously, renders those branches of government—or at very least the individuals who head up each branch who have personal knowledge of these crimes—complicit after-the-fact in those documented offences, many of which come under the reporting obligations of the respective *Criminal Justice Acts*.

5. THE CASE FOR A 'PART 2 ENQUIRY' BY THE HOUSES OF THE OIREACHTAS

Notwithstanding the unambiguous terminology that renders all citizens and residents of this State "subject to the law and the constitution", it is now a recognised fact amongst many thousands of Court users, that the application of the law to any particular individual in Ireland is almost entirely contingent on one's local social standing, on one's position within the machinery of State and/or on one's political connectedness – rather than on any genuine concept of 'the Rule of Law'. Perhaps this is why all of the authorities approached to date have reverted to frantic 'ostriching' or 'stonewalling' – once they realised that the usual obfuscation, intimidation, persecution and reprisals were just not working.

The 2020 I-I Report has proven beyond any reasonable doubt that the Irish Courts are giving preferential (and often prejudicially-unlawful) treatment to persons acting in an Official Capacity, and in doing so the Irish Courts are not meeting the requirements of Article 13 of the European Convention of Human Rights which requires *"an effective remedy before a national authority notwithstanding that the violation has been committed by persons acting in an official capacity."*

The Report also lists a number of Irish Officials and office holders who consequently engaged in those unlawful refusals of service; in obfuscation, obstructionism and stonewalling and, as-and-when that failed, the cowardly DPP reprisals began again. This is a morally-repugnant state of affairs and must be addressed by the incoming government as a matter of great and critical urgency. For to fail to do so is to fail those who have suffered so much already, and who have exhausted all other remedies in their desperate and wretched approaches to the State.

The *Houses of the Oireachtas (Inquiries, Privileges and Procedures) Act 2013* provides the Irish Government with the tools and authority to enquire into 'specified matters' including the conduct of Irish officials and office holders, and; *"a committee may conduct an inquiry into the removal or proposed removal of an officeholder (howsoever described) pursuant to a relevant provision."* Naturally, "a relevant provision" (howsoever described) would absolutely *have to* include the law of the land, given the requirement that all citizens and residents of the State are, "subject to the law and the Constitution". Indeed, the subsection following the above quote articulates some of those provisions and Office Holders that are explicitly referenced in the I-I Report. They include the power to remove from office the following office holder(s) for stated, "incapacity or misconduct":

The President (Pt 2,Ch.2 S.16) / Judges / the Comptroller and Auditor General / Officers of GSOC / Complaints Referee / the Ombudsman / Chairman of Dáil Éireann / the Clerk of Dáil Éireann / the Clerk of Seanad Éireann / the Information Commissioner / the Languages Commissioner / Members of the Ombudsman Commission / Broadcasting Authority (etc)...

As to whether the conditions of, "incapacity or misconduct" have been met, the reader is respectfully referred back to the I-I Report, *"Criminality in the Irish Courts, and the absence of the Rule of Law",* where all of us, including senior office holders appointed by Government are subject to the Rule of Law (at least theoretically) and it is upon this fundamental position and upon the more specific arguments herein that we ground this formal proposal and indeed make lawful, respectful demand of the Irish Government that they initiate *Part 2 Chapter 1 Enquiries* under the said *2013*

Act into; (i) the legal status and efficacy of the nation's Courts; and (ii) into the behaviour and conduct of those officials and office holders named in pages 235-239 of the I-I Report including the consequent detrimental effects on their respective Offices. This would require bringing *Article 35.4(i) Motions* as against any judges so named, and an *Article 12.10(i) Part 2, Chapter 2, S.16 Enquiry* into the unlawful and unconstitutional conduct— by omission or commission—of the incumbent President of Ireland.

The fact is, that we have an utterly untenable set of circumstances, where not only is the legal-constitutional validity of certain institutions of State under serious question; but the specific legal, moral and technical authority of the Courts is being grossly undermined and jeopardised by the actions of rogue and dishonest judges sufficient to render particular Courts at specific times absolutely and utterly 'unfit for purpose'.

When the Courts (and judges) so specified include several senior judges of the Superior Courts including the Supreme Court itself, then clearly we have a serious national problem – indeed a veritable constitutional crisis – which needs to be addressed with the utmost urgency if Ireland is to maintain any shambling pretence at democracy or adherence to the Rule of Law.

The Irish State now finds itself in a precarious position as to its ongoing sovereign status within the United Nations and as a Member-State of the European Union and the Council of Europe, given the requirements that Member States; (i) respect the Rule of Law, and (ii) have a properly-functioning justice system; neither of which in actual effect—not in function nor in practice—are fixed operational realities in this State.

6. THE CASE FOR THE ESTABLISHMENT OF THE PEOPLES TRIBUNAL OF IRELAND (PTI)

In seeking some sort of rational, credible and logical explanation for all of the routine contempt for the law and the Constitution ongoing in our Courts; for the repeat failures and refusals of any-and-all of the officials and office holders approached to date to respond in any meaningful way; and, whilst eliminating the implausible possibility that all of this routine malfeasance, obfuscation and stonewalling was merely the unfortunate result of truly astonishing levels of incompetence and stupidity and of ignorance of the law amongst some of the highest-placed legal professionals in the State; we have accordingly, arrived at the sorry but obvious conclusion that these illicit, unlawful and disingenuous activities are in fact, deliberate, conscious and knowing violations of the law which are being committed with scienter and malintent, in concert with others under the protection of superiors, by various agents of the State and by 'Officers of the Court' including by named judges.

In other words, and as expounded upon in more detail in the I-I Report, our Courts and our judges are not only NOT doing their jobs properly – they are in many cases doing exactly the opposite inasmuch as they are perverting, interfering with and obstructing justice – and are doing so with the active knowledge and support of their colleagues and subordinates. In doing so they bring shame and disrepute to their noble professions, and disgrace upon themselves. They also render the legal validity, the statutory authority and the Constitutional jurisdiction of those Courts utterly null-and-void by their actions. And meanwhile, where is *public* justice? No different to the rogue mechanic who damages cars instead of repairing them or who makes up invented problems so as to charge illicit workshop fees, any 'Officer of the Court' who defies or undermines genuine justice through dishonest means – and especially if he is doing so with a group of collaborators for devious, criminal ends. Well, what else should we call them other than a bunch of criminals! This in turn begs the thousand-dollar question: what are we supposed to do when a proven criminal with high statutory standing and authority gives us orders that we know are illicit, unlawful, detrimental or just plain wrong!?

As luck would have it, we do have an answer to that very question at hand. Because it has already been endorsed by all respective authorities in the existing 'QTC Notices' that NO resident or citizen—and most especially, NO civil or public servant—is obliged to acknowledge or obey unlawful instructions, no matter who that person is (or indeed how scary they look). Consequently, there is no statutory, legal or moral obligation on any resident or citizen of this State to engage with the said persons. Indeed, it may be a criminal offence in its own right for any such subordinate person to comply.

Accordingly, this Declaration places all Irish authorities officially 'On Notice' of the unlawful status of a number of senior officials and office holders so complicit, and by association, their *de facto* abandonment of tenure of their respective Offices. Naturally, this creates a certain void in the statutory operations of the State – most notably in the justice-related arena, as we await an urgent remedial response in the form of a *Part 2 Enquiry* by the newly-appointed Government. *(See p. 267).*

Based on our collective experiences at hundreds of court appearances and with scores of different judges (and with all due respect to those judges NOT of our experience who may in fact actually endeavour to respect their oaths of office) we hereby declare and assert our inalienable right under International, EU and domestic Irish Law to provide to the Irish public, 'a competent domestic tribunal' that will serve the interests of justice in Ireland to the limits of its power and authority in accordance with law; in alignment with *the Bangalore Principles of Judicial Conduct*; and according to the respective European Courts of Justice criteria; which said independent institution 'The Peoples' Tribunal' will be staffed by experienced, qualified experts in various fields for the purposes of establishing 'legal certainty' through the issuance of legally-binding rulings, findings and decisions. These mandates will be based precisely and literally on existing positive law, and will therefore have the *prima facie* force and authority of law.

The legal basis for the establishment of this independent body rests primarily (albeit partially) on:

(i) The various declarations of universal fundamental human rights which are binding on the Irish State but which are nevertheless being systematically flouted or ignored by agents and agencies of the State;

(ii) The repeat failures and refusals of all of the statutory authorities approached to date to honour and respect those fundamental rights;

(iii) The proofs of multiple criminal offences being committed by the said agents and agencies and the combined failure and refusal of the Irish authorities to apply the law;

(iv) The existence of – and the continuous production of – various disingenuous, misleading and calculatedly-deceptive documentation issuing out of the nation's Courts which variously cannot and do not stand up to even the most cursory alignment with the truth, with the evidence and/or with existing law;

(v) The unexplained disappearance of, and the unlawful suppression and/or amendment of documents (for illicit and unlawful purposes) that were validly submitted to the Courts;

(vi) The need for a competent, independent authority to provide lawful, truthful and wherever possible, incontestable judgments and rulings based purely on the texts of existing law;

(vii) The need for authentic and tangible recognition of the person's fundamental right to access justice as guaranteed by *Article 6 of the ECHR* and in particular, *"the right that litigants should have an effective judicial remedy enabling them to assert their civil rights according to the Rule of Law"*. [*ECtHR: Beles & others v. the Czech Republic, 2002*]

The PTI as 'A Competent Domestic Tribunal'.
As noted in our critique of the Irish Courts, the European Court of Justice has established 6 criteria for the recognition of 'a competent domestic tribunal' which we quote again here as inherent qualifiers for the formal recognition of the PTI – especially in circumstances where it has been demonstrated that the Rule of Law is NOT being respected or applied with any measure of consistency by the institutions of the Irish State.

1. The PTI has been 'established by law': This rests on three pertinent facts and circumstances. First of all, *Article 40.6 of the Irish Constitution* allows for freedom of expression, opinion and association. Secondly, and concomitantly, the parties responsible for the setting up and establishment of the PTI do NOT require permissions or licences from the Irish State to do so notwithstanding the explicit provision in *Article 37.1.* for the setting up of 'other judicial bodies'. Thirdly, and perhaps most importantly, all Irish authorities and senior office holders were placed formally 'On Notice' of the proposed establishment of the PTI complete with the PTI Mission Statement and a copy of the I-I Report containing all of the reasoning and grounds for the same. Each was given an opportunity to raise any lawful objections they might have. They have not done so. Accordingly, and in specific context of the Irish establishment's longstanding application of the puerile tactics of persistent stonewalling and obfuscation – those cowardly twin intangibles – so frustrating to have to deal with and so blatantly contemptuous of those with legitimate and often life-changing concerns which can only be addressed by 'the authorities'.. that in light of their collective failures and refusals to respond as requested, that the Peoples Tribunal of Ireland has now acquired additional (albeit unnecessary) 'official' legal legitimacy and standing from the Irish State according to the specific terms of the PTI Mission Statement which was formally served upon them 'On Notice' and 'under seal' under the long-established and widely-recognised legal principle, *"qui tacet consentire videtur"* – silence implies consent. *(See I-I Report pp.220-225)*

2. The 'permanence' of The Peoples' Tribunal of Ireland is established; (i) by virtue of having a permanent address for the receipt of correspondence and for the holding of meetings and hearings, which functions may also be taken 'on circuit' to other locations or, conducted online as the situation and circumstances require. (ii) The PTI is also now 'permanent' inasmuch as it will continue operations in Ireland under the direction and governance of the PTI Council until such time as it can be demonstrated to all concerned that; (a) the Rule of Law has been properly and statutorily established in this State; (b) that there is no further need for the independent oversight functions provided by the PTI; and (c) that the PTI Council acknowledges the same.

However, in objective consideration of the current scale and depth of 'official wrongdoing' within the organs of the State, it is clear that if we are to maintain any semblance of sovereign legitimacy or national dignity that *some* organised body with the characteristics as outlined in the PTI Mission Statement *must* be urgently convened. It must further be realistically anticipated that inasmuch as the PTI will represent, 'truth, justice and transparency' on behalf of the Irish people, that the PTI may indeed become a valuable—if not indeed an indispensible asset and a partner—to any genuine attempts by struggling public bodies to understand or adhere to the Rule of Law.

3. The 'compulsory jurisdiction' of the PTI rests primarily upon *Articles 37.1* and *40.6 of the Constitution*, and, somewhat ironically, upon the 'intrinsic vested jurisdiction' of the Rule of Law itself. Basic 'jurisdiction' (i.e. the permission and authority) to form and operate the PTI as a self-regulating body is ours by virtue of our inalienable right to free speech. The added jurisdiction to operate as 'a judicial entity' and/or as 'an association or union' is provided for in the Constitution.

> *Article 37.1. "Nothing in this Constitution shall operate to invalidate the exercise of limited functions and powers of a judicial nature, in matters other than criminal matters, by any person or body of persons duly authorised by law to exercise such functions and powers, notwithstanding that such person or such body of persons is not a judge or a court appointed or established as such under this Constitution."*

Article 40.6.(i) & (iii): "The State guarantees liberty for the exercise of the following rights, subject to public order and morality: – (i) The right of the citizens to express freely their convictions and opinions. (iii) The right of the citizens to form associations and unions.

'Compulsory jurisdiction' in the form discussed earlier suggests that either; (i) the PTI must have formal authority bestowed upon it by an Act of the Oireachtas (for example); and/or (ii) that the public (or other entities of the State) are lawfully *obliged* to comply with the PTI's Rulings and Findings. Very interestingly, both of these interpretations are expressly qualified (somewhat ironically) first of all, by the State's 'QTC' refusal to object to the setting up of the PTI which failure granted us the 'official authority' to do so – if such were so required; and secondly, by the fact that the PTI will ONLY be making rulings or judgments strictly according to the written Rule of Law which is of course vested with its own 'intrinsic jurisdiction'. In other words, and failing the occasional error-in-law that might occur (and for which unlikely circumstance the PTI Rules allow for corrections and amendments) any formal Findings or Rulings that issue out of the Adjudicating Division of the PTI will always and in every instance only quote written 'positive' law sources in strict order of legal authority. In other words, inasmuch as the law itself has intrinsic jurisdiction that demands compulsory acknowledgment and obedience, then so will any formal Rulings of the PTI demand lawful recognition; which said lawful recognition, in turn, establishes its 'compulsory jurisdiction'. The seemingly-prohibitive reference in *Article 37.1* to 'a judge or court not dealing with criminal matters' refers solely to *the imposition* of criminal penalties, because the *initiation* of criminal prosecutions remains a general right under *the Petty Sessions Act.*

An important distinction needs to be made between the concept of 'compulsory jurisdiction' and that of 'enforcement powers' by which a Court (for example) enforces its Orders by directing gardaí to take someone to jail or when a judge orders bailiffs to take someone's house. And this is where two of the most glaring anomalies of the Irish justice system repeatedly surface; (a) when an official or office holder deploys 'enforcement powers' when they have absolutely no jurisdiction to do so; and (b) when the same officials unlawfully *refuse* to employ their jurisdiction according to the Rule of Law. To put it more plainly, there couldn't be any *compulsory* enforcement of the law without the threat of jail or fines, and without some 13,000 gardaí ready to jump to a judge's command for example. Rogue judges are thus almost entirely dependent on the unquestioned obedience of gardaí, security, and Courts Service staff to enforce directions from the Bench – even when there may be no legal validity to those directions.

This is why *Article 37.1.* makes a distinction between civil and criminal matters, and why the only course of action for the PTI in the case of needing to 'enforce' its Rulings will be to return to the establishment by way of approaching the Garda Síochána, the Courts or the Government with Rulings and Findings that will oblige them under the law, to act according to the Rule of Law. The open publication of the same Rulings and Findings – especially if picked up by the mainstream media – may also serve to encourage and promote the appropriate, lawful responses by the statutory authorities, including by the enforcement arms of the State; An Garda Síochána, the DPP's Office and the Criminal Courts (no pun intended). This is NOT to say however, that any and all individuals who are members of the PTI do not still have full residual jurisdiction and authority to; (i) deploy existing powers of citizen's arrest, and/or; (ii) lodge 'common informer' applications in their own names for criminal summonses under *the Petty Sessions Act* as per paragraph '(v)' in the PTI Mission Statement.

4. The PTI will have *fair and equitable* 'inter partes' procedures according to the Rule of Law.

5. The PTI will apply rules of law in strict accordance with written 'positive' law. In particular, the PTI will NOT indulge in unnecessary convoluted legalese; it will NOT entertain unsubstantiated hearsay or any materials in evidence that are not factual and self-evident; and will NOT generate 'opinions' *per se* other than qualified explicatory commentary by the adjudicators (on the PTI website) on any apparent conflicts between aspects of law that do not have a clear order of supremacy.

6. Independence. Notwithstanding the liberty of any and all individuals, agencies or institutions whether private, commercial and/or statutory, to avail of the resources and published Rulings of the Peoples Tribunal according to standard PTI procedures; the PTI will remain completely independent of the State, of politics and of vested interests. In short, and inasmuch as it is capable of doing so, the PTI intends to provide to the Irish people a model of legal integrity and judicial propriety such as to set the standard for our beleaguered justice system.

Closing: For the avoidance of any doubt or confusion, and in the event we may have inadvertently misinterpreted or misunderstood the respective legislation, or otherwise breached or overlooked some pertinent issue or law; and, in the overall interests of transparency and accountability, we hereby invite the various officials and office holders who may be named in the I-I Report, *"Criminality in the Irish Courts and the*

Absence of the Rule of Law" or who are otherwise affected by the existence and proposed actions of the Peoples' Tribunal to respond to this Declaration with any observations, commentaries, suggestions or objections you may have to the continuation of The People's Tribunal of Ireland as outlined herein and as referenced in the said I-I Report, noting (respectfully) that we cannot and will not accept any generic or unsigned responses which do NOT address the crucial underlying question as to where the public are supposed to go for redress or remedy when there is so much evidence of unchallenged criminal wrongdoing; of contempt for the Rule of Law; of dishonesty, collusion, perjury and fraud in the Courts; as well as specific unlawful violations (by commission or omission) of their constitutional oaths or terms of office by the preeminent authority figures in this State, particularly in the period March 2011 to January 2020 and most notably by the incumbents of the following offices and institutions:

- The Office of the President of Ireland.
- The Office of the Taoiseach.
- Specific Council of State Members including the Attorney General.
- The Irish Government – and particularly the last three Ministers for Justice.
- The Association of Judges of Ireland – and several named members of the judiciary including the Presidents of all five Courts in the period February 2012 – July 2019.
- The Bar Council – and several named Barristers.
- The Office of the DPP, including the Director, the Chief Prosecuting Solicitor and other senior staff members as named in the I-I Report.

- Certain persons in the employ of the Chief State Solicitor's Office (CSSO).
- The Law Society of Ireland – and numerous named members of the solicitors' profession.
- The Irish Human Rights Commission, and the Chairwoman in particular.
- The Office of the Ombudsman.
- The Child and Family Agency (TUSLA) and the respective Ministers in charge.
- The Courts Service – and numerous named employees including current and previous CEO's.
- An Garda Síochána – and several named members of various ranks including Commissioners.
- The Garda Síochána Ombudsman Commission (GSOC).

In conclusion: it is sincerely hoped and expected that the labours of the Peoples Tribunal—albeit being an independent non-statutory body—will be welcomed by the Irish Establishment and by legal professionals and by honest and conscientious members of the judiciary in particular, given the documented dearth of intelligible outcomes to so many issues, disputes and cases being brought before the Irish Courts. It is hoped that the arrival of a genuinely independent body that is publically committed to truth, honesty and integrity; to genuine service of the people; and to providing legal clarity and certainty for those institutions of the State who are clearly struggling with the concept; that this will surely receive a warm and enthusiastic welcome on the national stage.

Despite the said 'limited powers of compulsory enforcement', *The Peoples' Tribunal of Ireland* can and will serve the Irish State and its people during any period of necessary reorganisational reform by providing for those essential justice-related services that are due to the people which are essential to good governance, and which said crucial services—currently effectively absent in any consistent or reliable form in this State—are incumbent on the Government to provide to the people, under the Rule of Law.

That in the continued absence, failures and/or refusals of the Irish Government to provide those services and guarantees under the Rule of Law, then it rests upon the residents and citizens of this State to lawfully provide for the same, or, to fail in their moral and patriotic duty.

We believe that the incoming Irish Government must now act with all due diligence in addressing what we have shown and demonstrated to be, 'a crisis of criminality in our Courts' and that the particular circumstances as outlined in the full published I-I Report [ISBN: 978-1-906628-88-8] clearly warrant an immediate and unqualified *Part 2 Enquiry* by *Dáil Éireann* under the terms of *the Houses of the Oireachtas (Inquiries, Privileges and Procedures) Act 2013.*

We hereby swear to the truth and the contents of this Declaration and appeal to the Irish Government in the form of the respective Committee(s), TD's, and/or Ministers of State to enquire without delay into the matters raised herein with a view to taking the appropriate action under the Rule of Law.

Thank you for your time and consideration.

Signed / Authorised etc.

PTI Executive, July 2020
On behalf of the PTI Council

SUPPLIMENTARY COMMENTARY BY THE PTI

The Solicitors, Barristers & Judges Franchise

"Judges must have at least 10 years' experience as a barrister or solicitor before being appointed to the District Court and at least 12 years' experience before being appointed to the High Court, the Court of Appeal or the Supreme Court."

Citizen's Information.ie, July 2020

By law, and according to the judge's constitutional oath, judges must be independent and impartial. But the reality on the ground is that control of the Irish Courts has been consigned to a collection of lawyers and judges who effectively operate as a national *franchise*, i.e. *"An authorization granted by a government (or company) to an individual or group enabling them to carry out specified commercial activities."*

Franchises operate under business rules for commercial gain. Courts are supposed to be in the business of justice. Yet the Courts Service, a commercial operation listed on the Companies Register states that it is, *"funded by the Irish State"* yet holds Court Funds of 2 Billion which are managed by an Investment Committee that is chaired by the President of the High Court. The Courts Service Board likewise, carries a majority of judges who are responsible for the overall management of the Courts despite their purported 'statutory independence'. These are the people who make up the Court Rules that will apply when they switch from their franchise-related duties to the business of delivering justice. And make no mistake, a business—and a very profitable one at that—it most certainly is; at least, for those inside the franchise.

This Benchers / Bar Association / Law Society / Courts

Service & Department of Justice franchise thus controls all aspects of the delivery of justice in Ireland – and all of the members of the franchise know their place and role.

Solicitors and Barristers who come before the Court are obliged to defer to judges – and judges expect the same. The question arises however, is this a business franchise, or, are we genuinely in the business of delivering justice?

Most litigants, completely unaware of this unacknowledged franchise, come before the Courts with naive notions of justice, not realising that they are greatly disadvantaged from the start and, despite their lawful entitlement to, *"an effective remedy before a fair and impartial tribunal"* that their chances of this rely almost entirely upon the proper application of EU Law, which frankly, is rarely in the interests of the Irish franchisees.

Unfortunately for the franchisees; Irish citizens voted in the Lisbon Treaty to make the Irish Courts and the Bar Association subject to and dependent upon European Law. But certain parts of EU Law that apply to human rights in particular are inconvenient to the Irish franchise, which is why we see Irish judges so often subverting or ignoring EU Law. This of course, is technically 'unlawful'.

Somewhat ironically, the combination of the supremacy of EU Law and the unlawful resistance of the Irish Courts franchise to defer to the same, provides not only the opportunity, but the necessity for the establishment of a national Court which acknowledges and applies EU Law.

Furthermore, and in light of the open defiance of the State to matters and policies that have been deemed 'unlawful' by the EU including; VRT (excise duty); the (no jury) Special Criminal Courts; the protection of tax loopholes for multinational corporations; Ireland's carbon emissions failures; and the political appointment of judges for example; there is also the deliberate misinterpretation of important EU Directives so as to *protect* corporate operations and vested interests including the misuse of GDPR to *enforce* secrecy; the contrived application of anti-discrimination laws; and the neutralisation of anti-corruption legislation that might otherwise see Irish office holders being held to account.

Article 6.1 of the Constitution is unambiguous. *"All powers of government, legislative, executive and judicial, derive, under God, from the people, whose right it is ..to decide all questions of national policy.."* The Irish People voted for membership of the European Union and for the fundamental rights expressed in the *European Convention of Human Rights Act 2003.* The PTI will provide the Irish public with 'legal certainty' according to EU and ECHR Law, whilst simultaneously highlighting the demise of an outdated franchise, political in essence, which urgently needs to align itself with the democratic wishes of the people, and update its operations and mechanisms to properly reflect the progress being made in the global quest for genuine, collective, social justice.

The PTI will be a direct asset to the Irish State in specific context of EU Law inasmuch as it will comprise qualified professionals in various fields, each experts in their own right. The PTI will produce short, succinct and clear Rulings in accordance with EU Law under the guidance of these experts, including internationally-trained lawyers.

The invitation remains open to any professionals in any field – or indeed to any persons with knowledge or experience that will help the Tribunal in its work, to contact the PTI to see where they might help to ensure that Ireland maintains its place as a modern democratic republic with a properly-functioning justice system that genuinely respects the human rights of its own people.

QTC 4' NOTICE & DECLARATION

*This formal Notice & Declaration is hereby served on all Irish authorities July 1st 2020

1. As an elected Official and/or Office Holder of this State I acknowledge that the sovereignty of the Irish State and its continued membership of the United Nations, the European Union and the Council of Europe is predicated on the genuine statutory adherence of the institutions of the Irish State with the Rule of Law.

2. I further acknowledge the statutory obligation on all Irish officials and office holders to carry out their official functions and duties in full accordance with the law and the Constitution.

3. I acknowledge receipt of the condensed version of the 2020 Report by the *Integrity Ireland Association* entitled, *"Criminality in the Irish Courts – and the absence of the Rule of Law"* and of the self-evident contents therein.

4. Inasmuch as the said Report documents the activities of listed officials and office holders; I recognise that the sum contents of the said Report indicates serious, repeat, critical failures by the said named persons to comply with their statutory obligations to respect the Rule of Law.

5. I acknowledge in particular the evidence of repeat, systemic, criminal activities by some named accused, many of whom hold high office in Government and in the Courts, and of the parallel

failures of the justice system to hold the said persons accountable according to Law.

6. I acknowledge the ineluctable truism; that of the consequent, collective and cumulative, systemic-and-endemic failures of the respective associated offices and institutions, to adhere to the Rule of Law.

7. I concur that Ireland *must* have an authentic, functioning justice system complete with valid domestic Courts established under law as per *Articles 34-38 of the Constitution,* and as per the 6-point criteria established by the ECJ.

8. That inasmuch as individual officials and/or office holders are clearly engaged in dishonest, unethical, amoral, unjust or unlawful activities, that such would render their tenure unconstitutional and invalid and would comprise grounds for referral to the *Houses of the Oireachtas* either for impeachment under *Article 35.4 of the Constitution* and/or for a *'Part 2 Enquiry'* under the terms of *the Houses of the Oireachtas (Inquiries, Privileges and Procedures) Act 2013* and that I support and endorse any such initiative on the basis of the evidence contained—or referred to—in the said *Integrity Ireland Report*.

9. That in the interim, and so as to provide for the criteria for continued membership of the United Nations, the Council of Europe and the European Union and so as not to compromise the status of Ireland as a sovereign nation-state nor render it

defunct and obsolete due to the proven absences of; (i) the Rule of Law and, (ii) a properly-functioning justice system; I hereby endorse and support the establishment of the *Peoples' Tribunal of Ireland* as per the terms laid out in the provisional 'PTI Mission Statement' in additional context of the 21-page *I-I Declaration* accompanying; to continue in open collaboration and cooperation with lawfully-established and properly-functioning institutions of the Irish State, until such time as the proper establishment of an authentic justice system complete with lawful, competent and independent Courts.

10. That if I am aware of any *lawful* objections or impediments to the immediate establishment of the *Peoples' Tribunal of Ireland* – complete with the authorities, powers and jurisdictions as laid out in the said PTI Mission Statement – that I will formally advise and inform the record of any such lawful impediments before close of business on or before July 7th 2020 complete with my own proposals (as an incumbent office holder) as to how to address the current absence of the Rule of Law in this State, and I undertake to return the same in writing to the PTI Executive or, that I surrender the opportunity to do so according to the legal principle, *"qui tacet consentire videtur"* – (silence implies consent).

Print Name:_____

Office / Position:_____

Signed:_____Date:_____